DESTINATION BRANDING for SMALL CITIES

■

The Essentials for Successful Place Branding

SECOND EDITION
Completely Revised and Expanded

DESTINATION BRANDING for SMALL CITIES

▪

The Essentials for Successful Place Branding

SECOND EDITION
Completely Revised and Expanded

Bill Baker

Destination Branding for Small Cities
The essentials for successful place branding

SECOND EDITION
Completely Revised and Expanded

Published by:
Creative Leap Books
20212 SW 86th Ave.
Portland, Oregon 97062 USA

Printed in the United States of America

Cover Design: Mike Winder, Next Level Graphics, Portland

ISBN 13: 978-0-9849574-0-8

ISBN 10: 0-9849574-0-5

LCCN: 2012930054

Contents

Praise for the First Edition of Destination Branding for Small Cities

"Baker's writing style is engagingly direct and to the point, and his book should be essential reading for anyone involved in the study or implementation of city branding."

Journal of Brand Management

"For America to be globally competitive, our communities need to embrace the concept of branding for both tourism and economic development. The stronger they are, the stronger our Nation will become. Bill Baker has done a remarkable job of describing the process and making it easy to understand place branding. His chapters on subjects like "What's Your Place in the World" make it a mandatory read for economic development professionals and public officials interested in sustainable prosperity."

Ed Burghard, CEO and Manager,
Strengthening Brand America

"This book once and for all destroys the myths and misinformation surrounding the branding of places. It has the potential to save millions of dollars wasted by cities, states and nations on ill-conceived and ineffective campaigns purporting to be brand development exercises."

John King OAM, Chairman,
Australian Tourism Export Council

"There is an increasing realization of the important links between urban design and place branding. Bill's book has gone a long way in bridging the gap between the two. Combining the skills of placemaking through urban design expertise and the branding of cities and regions are of vital importance in the future. Bill's principles and guidelines apply to cities and regions in every country."

Odd Arne Blindheim, Chairman of the Board,
Nordic Urban Design Association

"Baker identified the prevailing conditions, which authorities must be aware of to realize their city brand ambitions. The book shared the author's expertise, richly illustrated with examples while focusing on concepts, tools and techniques that really matter to practitioners and civic leaders alike in a user-friendly way. Not only a great business read, but also a service to society."

Frank M. Go, Professor at Rotterdam School of Management, Erasmus University, The Netherlands

"I stopped highlighting Bill's book in the middle of Chapter Seven. The ink was running low and I realized pretty much all the information was relevant and deserving of emphasis. Bill's sense-of-place model to uncovering "who" Billings was, is and can be allowed us to build a brand that is uniquely our home."

John Brewer, President, Billings (MT) Chamber of Commerce

"Branding places is a unique and complex process due to the broad mix of stakeholders and the significantly different target audiences. Bill Baker has written a very useful book for those wishing to create more compelling place brands. He gives numerous examples of how they can apply sound branding principles to increase tourism and economic development. Anyone involved in promoting their community or region would benefit from reading this book before they commence the branding process."

Brad VanAuken, global brand consultant and author of *Brand Aid*

"In the last decade destination branding has become one of the most talked about concepts amongst place marketers but it still needs greater explanation. Bill Baker makes a major contribution to that task in this book that is hugely readable, yet immensely practical and readily communicates Baker's enthusiasm for and command of his subject. This book is set to become a must have for anyone involved in place marketing."

Prof. Nigel Morgan, Cardiff Metropolitan University, author of *Destination Branding*

"Bill Baker provides practical advice and examples of real world destination, of value to both practitioners and academic researchers. The new edition is a must have for anyone interested in the challenge faced by destination marketers."

Dr. Steven Pike, Senior Lecturer, Queensland University of Technology

"It is easy to recommend Bill Baker's book; his global experience is impressive. It outlines the practical thought process that any city leader can understand. It is very insightful and has a lot of successful case studies. Most importantly, this book details how to avoid wasting money on superficial advertising and promotion campaigns and focus on substance. It should be required reading for every city council, council member or county commissioner."

Duane Knapp, author of *The BrandPromise*®
and DMAI's *Destination BrandScience*

"The principles outlined by Baker have direct relevance to larger destinations, including nations. It could only have been written by someone with a lifetime of frontline experience in branding/marketing places of all sizes. You can see that Baker has worked all streams of the communications mix. It's a must read for every destination marketer."

Rodney Harrex, Regional Director,
UK/Europe, Tourism Australia

"This is an outstanding book, for large and small cities. It's also an excellent tool for a county or region. Baker's roadmap empowers a place of any size to distill its distinctive and genuine personality into a useful brand. I only wish I had had this tool 40 years ago."

Reyn Bowman, President Emeritus,
Durham Convention & Visitors Bureau

"Destination branding has reached a tipping point where everyone is talking about it – but so few are doing it well. Bill Baker has authored what I believe to be the finest treatise on the topic to date. Filled with case studies of both the good and the bad, *it* defines what destination brands are and aren't ... and outlines a clear path for cities that want to do it right."

Bill Geist, President,
Zeitgeist Consulting USA

"It's always a challenge to find curriculum material that's useful for my students who will seek employment in small cities. Prior to this book I was stuck with academic textbooks full of research on major global destination cities only. Baker's book is ideal because it exposes students to the real world situations and challenges they will find, and the solutions they will have to employ."

Eric Aebi, Lead Instructor, Hospitality & Tourism
Management, Chemeketa Community College

"Today's technology and mobility make it essential for all cities to establish a strong brand as a unifying focus for public, private and non-profit organizations. Baker's book is an authoritative guide to understanding the branding process and the importance of giving your brand life. It's an easy read, concise, and filled with helpful hints and case studies. A must read for every DMO."

Andrew Alberti, Program Manager,
Lakes to Locks Passage All-American Road

"This book is straight to the point and an accessible strategy guide. Despite, dealing with a whole country, for me the book has been a perfect fit because all places have the same complexities, whether cities, counties or countries. The book can be a great inspiration to everyone interested in the subject, taking its first steps or dealing with it on a daily practice."

Inga Hlín Pálsdottir,
Director, Marketing & Visit Iceland at Promote Iceland

"Why pay a university thousands of dollars to take a branding class when this book sums it up together incredibly well. Baker has thought of all facets of destination branding, and most importantly, through the eyes of smaller destinations, which often don't have the staff or financial resources to make things happen. This should be required reading and is relevant to cities and areas worldwide."

Erik Wolf, President and CEO,
International Culinary Tourism Association

"Bill's book is an absolute necessity for small cities looking to brand their destinations. It should be given to all stakeholders prior to beginning any branding program to avoid the challenges many of us have faced along the way to a compelling brand."

Melyssa Laughlin, President,
Vacaville (CA) Conference & Visitors Bureau

"This isn't a book you read once. No matter where you are in the process of leading your community's branding, you need to go back to it regularly. For beginners, the book is essential to keep you focused on the right path and ensuring that you aren't taking a detour. After years into our community's process, I find inspiration and energy by reading it through again. If this work starts to become second nature, beware. It's time to re-read and get a refresher on the basics."

Jim Epperson, CDME. President/CEO,
Harrison County Convention & Visitors Bureau

Acknowledgements

Destination Branding for Small Cities evolved as a result of my being at the forefront in place and destination marketing and branding for four decades. My journey began in Australia's Hunter Valley which is today one of the world's great wine tourism destinations. Then, for more than a decade, I was fortunate to be engaged in developing and implementing Australia's brand strategies in 26 countries, which was possibly the finest learning opportunity any place marketer could be given. This included launching Australia's award winning and acclaimed "*Shrimp on the Barbie*" campaign in the USA and Canada, which I managed for seven years. This was one of the pioneering efforts in branding a country and allowed me to shape many of the ideas and techniques that are in this book.

Over the past twenty years, the journey has taken me to hundreds of locations in the USA, Australia, Canada, and many other countries. Working as a consultant or keynote speaker in these locations enabled me to gain an even greater appreciation for the challenges faced by cities when it comes to honing their competitiveness

During my career there have been many people who deserve my thanks for their expert advice, friendship and encouragement. I have had the privilege of working with and learning from some of the most talented place and destination marketing and branding experts in the world. The list of their names is far too long to mention each one.

My gratitude to the great people from the worldwide offices of the Australian Tourist Commission (now Tourism Australia) and its outstanding advertising and research agencies, and my friends in the North American, European and Australian travel industries. My special thanks go to our clients, who have encouraged Total Destination Marketing to always be innovative and on the leading edge. These opportunities have exposed me to the thinking and techniques that are the foundation of this book.

I was surprised and delighted with the international acclaim the first edition of this book received. Noting the feedback has encouraged me to expand the subjects in this edition.

My wife and business partner Joan deserves special thanks for her encouragement and amazing attention to the quality of this book. Our daughters Renee and Kate are my inspiration, and I hope that this book can contribute in a small way to making a better world for them to discover and explore.

Bill Baker

Preface

Small cities around the world are recognizing that place branding directly contributes to increased effectiveness and efficiency in how cities compete and present themselves. It enables the city to focus on their differentiating strengths and leverage the combined power of stakeholder resources to establish their competitive identity. Despite the many successes there are some failures that could have been avoided and this book presents many of the actions necessary to avoid some of the ever-present pitfalls.

This is the second edition of *Destination Branding for Small Cities* and is written as a primer to simplify and clarify the practice of branding small cities. It is designed to demystify what can be complex concepts and processes required to reveal a competitive brand identity that will be widely accepted by stakeholders, yet resonate strongly with target audiences.

This book is not an academic expose, nor does it contain all of the technical elements that may be needed for the branding of places with substantial research budgets. The branding of most small cities relies very heavily on hard-working people who may not have a degree in marketing, who depend on part-time and volunteer staff, and who often have limited resources to engage outside professional assistance. I have attempted to simplify the issues and suggest affordable, proven techniques that can be employed by destinations of all sizes.

This revised edition has retained the focus on the essentials, but has expanded its scope to more fully explore the creation of an overarching place brand in addition to a destination brand for tourism. The examples include places beyond the USA as a reflection of the international interest in the first edition. I have also included insights on important issues from my colleagues, some of whom are among the world's leading place branding specialists. They serve to demonstrate the universal application of the concepts and ideas.

I use the terms "destination," "community," "city," "location" and "place" interchangeably to refer to the geographical entity at the heart of the brand. I consider a 'destination' to be a place that people will leave their present location in order to visit, shop, invest, or relocate. After the first book's release in 2007, I received many comments from readers and colleagues around the world suggesting that the title should cover more than small cities because the book's point of view is relevant to places of all sizes, including countries. They are correct in that the principles are very similar, however I am aiming to provide details, nuances and approaches that are specific to small cities. While the title is *Destination Branding for Small Cities* the underlying principles and processes can just as readily be applied to regions, counties, byways, Main Streets, suburbs, and yes, even countries.

The book has proven to be particularly useful for public and non-profit organizations that must create a brand strategy through collaboration and consultation with multiple, diverse stakeholders, and within the confines of a limited budget. It is a hands-on toolkit designed to assist with brand development for communities with a population of fewer than 250,000 residents, although there is no fixed rule regarding city size. In most cases, cities of this size and smaller can't afford wide-ranging consumer research or high-profile advertising campaigns. Yet, there remains the need for them to be competitive in order to attract more visitors, talented people, inward investment, and new businesses. The processes, techniques and tools apply whether the strategy is for an overarching brand or more closely focused on tourism or economic development.

Readers of this edition of *Destination Branding for Small Cities* will find it useful as a:

- Source of practical information for branding places, particularly cities and regions.
- Roadmap to guide their brand planning.
- Resource to enhance brand knowledge within their organization and the community.
- A blueprint to introduce a stronger strategic focus to the presentation and competitiveness of the city.

The marketing and strategic planning capabilities of communities vary enormously according to their population, attractors, resources, market maturity, politics, public awareness, history, economic base, and marketing expertise. For instance, the Las Vegas Convention and Visitors Authority (LVCVA) has a marketing budget of more than $100 million per year with a worldwide reputation and a tourism infrastructure that is possibly the most developed and sophisticated in the world. The LVCVA budget is equal to the combined budgets of thousands of smaller American cities. This certainly does not mean that these smaller locations should wave white flags and give up trying to market themselves, but it *does* mean they must have a strong strategic focus to whatever they do – and don't do.

Recommending the practices of Las Vegas, Melbourne, and London to small cities is hardly appropriate. I have specifically designed this book for ambitious places that recognize that they must adopt a branded approach, despite having a modest budget. Relatively small cities such as Oshkosh WI, Todmorden (England), and Wollongong (Australia), along with hundreds of others, are doing excellent jobs in creating distinctive brands for themselves on more modest budgets.

I refer generically to the variety of organizations responsible for managing the city's brand planning as a destination marketing organization (DMO). This term is intended to embrace Convention & Visitor Bureaus, Chambers of Commerce, local government entities, downtown associations, Main Street associations, economic development authorities and other similar organizations.

Interesting examples are provided to illustrate specific brand issues and applications. Some of these places excel in one or more aspects of their branding, but my reference is not meant to infer that every aspect of their program is necessarily an excellent example of brand development. I also refer to some places that are not small cities. The reason for this is to demonstrate specific practices that are appropriate to places of all sizes.

The brand planning that you conduct for your city will be one of the most rewarding events in your career. It presents opportunities for learning and moving to new levels of effectiveness and efficiency, for uniting partners, and sharpening the city's competitiveness. Most of all, it should contribute toward the increased economic and social well-being of your community – and that will be the greatest reward of all.

Introduction

Close emotional ties exist between people and the places they live, visit and work. This brings an added dimension to consider when it comes to introducing practices such as place branding and marketing to a community. This is a reality that owners and marketers of consumer goods rarely face. Whether as residents or visitors, we have very special bonds to places and this can lead to a very tricky planning process.

Cities must constantly adjust to changing circumstances, all the while maintaining a balance with the values and vision of their residents. Those ambitious places wanting to increase their well-being and reputation through tourism and economic development should first answer some basic questions:

- What do we want to be known for?
- How can we stand out from the crowd and be more competitive?
- What thoughts and feelings do we want to come to mind when people are exposed to our name?
- How can we gain improved results from our resources?

These questions are at the heart of branding. To successfully answer them the city needs to be customer-focused, strategic, open-minded, and imaginative in order to reveal the brand in a way that will generate positive feelings, respect, and loyalty. It must be crystal clear about what it is, what it does, why it is interesting, and why it should matter to specific audiences.

Places are not homogenous. Branding these complex entities takes much more than a cookie cutter approach or an afternoon brainstorming session. What may work in revealing and building the brand for one place, may not necessarily work in another. The processes outlined herein provide tools that can be adapted to a variety of circumstances.

While branding has been applied to consumer products for decades, the concept of destinations and places formulating brand strategies only began to appear during the 1990s. A strategic approach to destination branding was first introduced at a national level. The nations of Australia, Hong Kong, and Spain were among the first to truly embrace the practice. It was then adopted by major cities such as Seattle, Las Vegas, and Pittsburgh who were among the early American adopters. These innovators introduced branding to compete more effectively in an increasingly competitive world, create a strategic decision-making framework, and to address the calls on behalf of stakeholders for increased accountability in the marketing of places.

According to Jeremy Hildreth, head of place branding at London agency Saffron, "We have a tendency to think of a city's star as permanently fixed, in reality the fortunes of places rise and fall over time. Our perceptions shift too, but they are imperfectly correlated with reality. We continue to think positively of a place even if it no longer deserves it. It seems we'll forgive a place anything provided it's sexy and going there gives us something to talk about when we get home. A city's brand is an overall image and set of associations that resides in people's heads and branding means the deliberate actions taken to alter or improve an image."[1]

Most forward thinking places now regard branding as an essential component of their tourism and community development toolkits. It has been elevated in importance to the point where Destination Marketing Association International (DMAI), the world's largest official destination marketing organization, has designated the development of a brand strategy as one of the critical items needed for accreditation in the Association's "Destination Marketing Accreditation Program."

While place branding is being successfully adopted around the world, there are some who mistakenly regard it as a fad. In examining their critique, I often find that they don't really understand the concept and often can't get much beyond the logo and tagline. They don't consider its benefits in providing a strategic framework. Malcolm Allan at Colliers International in London has an interesting perspective on this, "Place branding is a relatively new discipline and its small but growing band of adherents and practitioners have often been received with disdain and disbelief by people from established professions in town planning, economic development and tourism, numbers of whom regard it as a passing fad, just a new way of sexing-up traditional approaches to city planning, marketing and place making. As a qualified practicing town planner and economic development professional for over thirty years, I see it very differently. For me the key word is *strategy* as in place, city or development brand strategy. I have often been struck by the power of major lasting brands to meet the changing needs of their customers whilst remaining true to their purpose and values – they provide a much needed (and proven) strategic guidance system."

Realizing the power of a brand strategy to make their cities more competitive and successful, leaders are embracing the branding techniques that were once the domain of commercial products and services. Even so, not all place brands are successful. Too many fall short of their objectives. In the coming pages, I will address the common pitfalls and how to avoid them.

The thoughts and associations that come to mind when a city's name is heard or read can have huge financial, political, and social value. Too few city leaders think about the number of jobs, businesses, and other organizations that directly benefit from their city's image and reputation. The level of esteem that a city's name evokes has a direct impact on the health of its tourism, economic development, prestige, and respect. Unfortunately, a city's image and reputation often go largely unrecognized, unappreciated and unmanaged. They rarely get measured and never appear on a balance sheet or the job evaluation of a Mayor, City Manager or elected official. With so much riding on its image and reputation, it makes sense to have a strategy to nurture, manage, and protect these most valuable of city assets.

You've Got Company

The USA has approximately 20,000 cities, 3,400 counties, 126 America's Byways, and 12,800 designated National Historic Districts. That does not include the states, regions, resorts, and neighborhoods that are also clamoring for attention. No wonder most small and mid-sized cities find it hard to be seen and heard in this crowd! Then we can add thousands of cities, regions and destinations in other countries all wanting their share of global tourism, trade and talent.

It may be hard to believe that 90% of incorporated cities in the USA have a population of less than 50,000 residents.[2] Actually, 80% of them have less than 10,000 residents. This means that the struggle to gain attention is not limited to those with large populations and large marketing budgets. The "little guys" are also competing against other enterprising small cities in lower profile, but no less intense, battles with the prizes being more family wage jobs, new businesses, high-spending travelers and talented newcomers.

Today, cities of all sizes find themselves competing against places and organizations on the other side of the world. This global contest has brought even small-town America onto the radar of global corporations. At the same time, international visitors to countries worldwide have shown an increasing inclination to go beyond the traditional major gateway cities to discover more of the authentic, distinctive qualities in small cities and regions. This new paradigm means that ambitious communities must compete by using the same marketing and branding principles that were once the exclusive domain of corporations and nations.

Choice is not limited to the battle between one city and another. Locations within cities are also in fierce competition with each other, i.e. city centers vs. neighborhoods, big box retailers vs. Main Streets or High Streets, shopping malls vs. traditional downtowns, and suburbs competing with all of the above. We even find modern shopping centers in the suburbs that are built to look like traditional downtowns and Main Streets. Examples of this can be found at Bridgeport Village in Portland OR and The Streets at Southpoint in Durham NC. This heightened competitive environment makes it imperative for places, no matter their size or composition, to clearly differentiate themselves and convey why they are the most relevant and rewarding options.

We've all had the experience of discovering the reality of a place being different from the perceptions and expectations we hold. Those perceptions may have been shaped by our travel experiences, education, comments from friends and relatives, social media and even movies, books, songs, and television. A complex web of factors such as its distinctive location, geography, economy, climate, history, culture, religion or architecture has produced the city's actual character. The challenge for all communities is to bridge and manage the gap between the externally held perceptions and the reality of the place. Many are even trying to compete with an image that is out of date, inaccurate, or unbalanced.

To the annoyance of many city leaders, the commonly held view of their city may be out of sync with what they see as its reality. While the city may have invested millions of dollars in infrastructure projects, public works, promotions, urban design, and events, an outdated or bland image may still be widely held after many years of positive change within the community. This gap can mean lost income, jobs, tax revenues and reputation.

To the annoyance of many city leaders, the commonly held view of their city may be out of sync with what they see as its reality.

The biggest challenge that many places face is taking control of their identity and reputation which have been unmanaged for a long time. Without a brand strategy, a city may bounce from one set of images and associations to another without considering what the city should be known for.

Then there is the "blank slate" problem identified by Andy Levine, President of Development Counsellors International, who estimates that 70 to 80 percent of all cities in the U.S. have no dominant image at all in the public mind. Thus, finding a core differentiating asset, or 'unique selling proposition' as he terms it, becomes even more important.

Fortunately, communities are becoming increasingly conscious of the need to proactively shape and influence what the world thinks of them and to position and market themselves with strategic intent, not simply by what seems like a good idea at the time. An important starting point is for city leaders to recognize that there is a direct link between the city's image and reputation and its attractiveness as a place to visit, live, invest, and study. An even greater realization for some is that inaction is not a viable option if they genuinely want to improve local prosperity.

Malcolm Allan of Colliers International makes the point, "Competing on tax breaks, tax credits, free land, soft loans and other financial incentives to attract investors and to shore up local industries is a zero sum game and clearly a race to the bottom and one that is impossible to sustain. What is needed is a frank rethink about what the city offers of value and will offer in future. City branding is about being very strategic about the value and nature of the city's strengths and experience, both of which need to be distinctive, and then deliberately creating, developing and demonstrating their value through appropriate on-brand actions."

Successful place branding takes a concerted effort to attain a vision where the reality experienced by its customers matches the positive expectation or promise being conveyed by the city and its partners.

CHAPTER ONE

The World of Brands and Branding

Over-Supply and Overload

We are living in the most over-communicated period in history. On an average day Americans are bombarded by over 5,000 commercial messages in one way or another. Our lives are cluttered with an over-abundance of products, advertising, media choices, messages, and options. Products, whether they are coffee, automobiles, or cities, must somehow cut through this clutter and "noise" to connect with customers.

The reaction of many consumers to this overload is to block out these intrusions, as so many of us do with TiVo and pop-up blockers, in an effort to protect ourselves from unwanted messages. As marketers, this makes your task even more difficult and more expensive. Do you turn up the volume by placing more advertising? But what if you don't have a big advertising budget? Or should you play smarter and sharpen your messages to clarify what you stand for? Take a leaf from the most successful marketers of consumer goods who adopt a branded approach to consistently demonstrate how their products are distinctive, relevant, and meaningful. Branding is the most effective way to escape the sameness and blandness that is enveloping so many of your competitors.

It's easy to find look-alikes and knock-offs of watches, clothes, or even cities. Just take a look at the abundance of similar content in the websites of cities offering "me too" physical features and lists of things to do. Winning cities are those that break through the clutter to become well known and easily recognized because they stand for something special. They project irresistible reasons to think of them as being different and representing greater value than other choices.

In this era of super brands it may seem an unusual notion to consider a city, state, region or country as a brand. However, in the context of a *place* selling itself as a focal point to visit or to buy real estate, it makes sense that it should be managed as a brand in order to shape and control its competitive identity and to make choices easier for customers.

When asked whether it's possible to treat a complex entity such as a city or country as a brand, Landor UK managing director Charles Wrench told the BBC "Absolutely, they are brands. I would say that anything for which you can construct a mental inventory is a brand." [3]

Branding vs. Marketing

At times the terms 'branding' and 'marketing' are used interchangeably. This is a mistake as there are distinct differences. *Branding* provides the framework or organizing principles for focusing the city's competitive identity to convey and deliver on its distinctive and valued promise. Branding brings consistency to the experiences at every critical touchpoint with customers. In the case of place branding, this calls into play a wide range of partners, actions and disciplines. Not all of these elements are covered within marketing.

Marketing is defined by the American Marketing Association as "the activity, set of institutions, and processes for creating, communicating, delivering, and exchanging offerings that have value for customers, clients, partners, and society at large." [4] Marketing is conducted through what is referred to as the 4Ps, Product, Price, Promotion and Place, to reach and facilitate transactions with end consumers. The brand strategy and the brand platform elements (such as positioning, personality, key experiences and tone of voice) are at the heart of marketing and shape communications and the delivery of the brand promise.

Branding is long-term and strategic, while marketing is strategic (or at least should be) but is shorter-term and primarily tactical. Brands are distinctive, where marketing isn't. Marketing is an element of branding. Not the other way around. Marketing alone, cannot carry a place brand, even when you involve the 4P's. It doesn't sit neatly in only the marketing department or tourism office.

An overarching place (and even a destination) brand may involve urban planners, architects, city managers, government officials and others. Many more than would normally be the case with marketing. It might raise organizational, partnership, regulations, transportation, placemaking, government policies, education system and many more issues, including the success and celebrity of its citizens and events.

While not a city, Disney is an excellent example of a brand being central to everything they do. Their essence is "family freedom" and this is the beacon that guides everything from hotels, to theme parks, to cruise ships, and movies. It shapes their staff grooming policies, security services, recruitment and engineering. Mahesh Enjeti at SAI Marketing Counsel (Australia) captured this in saying, "A brand is not a function of marketing. It is the very foundation of your business."

Establishing the brand platform for a city precedes, and is central to its marketing.

Establishing the brand platform for a city precedes, and is central to its marketing. They are both reliant on each other and are certainly interconnected. The brand is integral and inseparable from the overall business strategies of the city's marketing portfolio, i.e. tourism, investment, relocation.

I recently had a conversation with the president of a DMO on the East Coast who was being pressured by some of his lodging partners because the city's brand strategy, revealed three months earlier, had not generated an increase in business for them. While we at TDM didn't develop this strategy, it did seem to be a fairly good one.

The partners need to remember that while there may be some short-term increases in visitation, the real benefits of branding won't be apparent overnight. If the partners wanted to increase heads in beds in the short-term, perhaps they should have invested more in their tactical marketing communications. It takes time to break through the competitive clutter to build awareness, and then to convert interest into actual business. They are mistaking the roles of branding and marketing. Branding requires a long-term strategic mindset, not just a short-term promotional outlook.

What *IS* a Brand?

Despite the wave of books, articles and fellow speakers on the subject, branding is still one of the most misunderstood concepts in business and government today. There are probably as many definitions of a brand as there are branding books. There is no single definition. Many people still don't grasp that it is much more than a logo, tagline, or advertising theme. Yes, I know. I sound like a broken record. But it's a perception that is seriously holding back true place branding and improved performance. I think of a brand as:

The totality of thoughts, feelings and expectations that form a distinctive and compelling promise and enables people to more easily choose one product or service over another.

In essence, the hallmark of a successful brand is determined by the value of the promises that it makes, and the promises that it keeps. A brand adds value, meaning and an invisible aura to a product or entity – even a generic product. Look in the produce section of your supermarket and you'll see oranges, bananas, and tomatoes all with stickers that proclaim a brand identity offering superior, yet intangible points of difference. Evian and Morton's have created powerful brands for commodities as basic as water and salt by promising intangible qualities that add value. We can consider a brand as being the difference between:

- A bottle of water and a bottle of Evian
- A cup of coffee and a cup of Starbucks
- An amusement park and Disneyland
- A hotel and The Four Seasons

A brand is not a physical entity – it exists only in the customer's mind. A brand is a collection of associations and thoughts that are stored in the minds of individuals and not simply the opinions and hopes of a committee or the marketing department. A true brand must make and keep a clear, single-minded promise and then consistently deliver on it.

What Is Place Branding?

After years of branding places of all sizes we have adapted the conventional definition of a brand to form the following:

***A place brand** is the totality of thoughts, feelings, and expectations that people hold about a location. It's the reputation and the enduring essence of the place and represents its distinctive promise of value, providing it with a competitive edge.*

***Place branding** provides a framework and toolkit for differentiating, focusing and organizing around the location's competitive and distinctive identity. It is grounded in truth and reality.*

Place branding provides a framework and toolkit for differentiating, focusing and organizing around the location's competitive and distinctive identity. It is grounded in truth and reality.

Despite their good faith and good intentions, cities can find developing a place brand challenging because it takes passion, commitment, innovation and, most importantly because no single entity owns the location. Therefore, a highly collaborative environment is required. Partners throughout the location must embrace the attitude that *each time* they are in touch with a customer is an opportunity to reinforce and build the brand through positive customer experiences or "vignettes" of the brand.

Effective brands make customer buying choices easier. They aim directly at our hearts because our emotions drive and initiate most, if not all, of our decisions, and then they provide the logic for us to rationalize our decision. The excellent brochures, packages and websites of Newport RI, Cancun (Mexico), and Queenstown (New Zealand) do a great job in engaging our senses and feelings and then winning over our logic.

What Are the Types of Place Brands?

Place brands can take several forms. Most are based on their geographic boundaries, while thematic brands relate to clusters which form themes that resonate with specific audiences. The common types of place brands are:

An overarching place brand is the overall, high level umbrella or parent brand embracing a city's holistic qualities. It captures the city's distinct personality and sense of place and usually includes the competitive identity for the city's marketing portfolios directed toward tourism, economic development, education, investment or community pride. Sometimes, an overarching place brand is simply referred to as a place brand. The term, 'place brand' is also used at times in the book to generically refer to the branding of locations. In these cases, the reference may be to the practice of developing a destination brand, an overarching place brand or a brand for relocation or education.

A destination brand refers to the brand in the context of the location being an attractive place to visit. It is sometimes referred to as a tourism brand. Cities often opt for a formalized destination or tourism brand rather than an overarching place brand because tourism may be the "loudest voice" and most organized in communicating its attributes. The tourism industry usually has the largest marketing budgets and need for conveying the city's attractiveness. A place brand should not be regarded as a replacement for a destination brand. There is still the need for a brand strategy that is specifically directed toward tourism markets. However, if the city has both a place and a destination brand there must be very close links between the two.

An economic development brand, not including tourism, is directed toward business relocation, expansion and investment. Like the destination brand, it requires a brand strategy separate, but linked, to the overarching brand to ensure that it has optimal potency with target audiences.

A community brand is created to resonate with local residents and is usually designed to boost local pride, provide a sense of identity for the place, or increase local patronage for residential, retail, entertainment, leisure and sporting activities.

Thematic brands can be founded on historical, wine, culinary, sporting or cultural themes. They might be present within one location or spread across a region or nation linking areas with the same strengths that are of interest to specific market segments. Examples of thematic brands include The Oregon Trail, England's Golf Coast and The Year of Alabama Food. It's possible for a city to have a place brand founded on its geographical boundaries and also be represented by a thematic brand. The Romantic Road (Germany), coined by travel agents in the 1950s to describe the 220 miles of highway in southern Germany, provides a good example. The area dates from mediaeval times and possesses classic German towns, scenery and culture. The route is also known for its castles, such as the famous Neuschwanstein Castle. While the brand equity of the Romantic Road is considerable, several of the towns along its route, such as Rothenburg, Wurzburg and Fussen have strong individual brand identities, even though they may have developed organically.

Small City Branding Around the World

United Kingdom: Keith Dinnie, Ph.D at Breda University of Applied Sciences (The Netherlands) and author of *Nation Branding – Concepts, Issues, Practice* and *City Branding* provides an overview of small city branding in the United Kingdom.

"As budgets come under increasing pressure, cities in the UK find themselves having to sharpen their focus on finding effective ways to collaborate with local stakeholders in order to achieve city branding goals such as tourism promotion and investment attraction. The collaborative imperative is particularly acute for small cities whose budgets do not allow for expensive national and international marketing campaigns. The English seaside town of Margate, for example, has adopted a strategy of stakeholder engagement in which partners such as the city council, regional and central government, and private sector partners work together to rejuvenate the image (and the reality) of a town that has been undergoing many years of regeneration. In addition to budgetary constraints, a major challenge for small cities in the UK lies in how to avoid being ignored in a year in which the English capital London will dominate media coverage even more than it normally does, due to its hosting of the 2012 Olympic Games. Creative ways are being explored in order for small UK cities to benefit from the global attention that is primarily focused on London. Despite the economic climate there is heightened awareness among small cities of the need to differentiate themselves and this is contributing toward the continued introduction of the principles of place branding."

Continental Europe: Robert Govers, Adjunct Professor at Leuven University (Belgium) and author of *Place Branding* and co-editor of the *International Place Branding Yearbook* series notes that the practice of city branding in Europe has created a very diverse landscape.

"Some cities believe that the design of a logo and slogan will change their image. Then there are those that hope they can build their reputation solely through communications campaigns. However, the cities that are often referred to as best-practice are very often revitalized second-tier cities that have rebranded their often industrial past with competitive identity strategies, clearly establishing brand purpose and promise, and focusing on strategy, policy, partnerships and symbolic actions with or without the support of a logo, slogan or communication campaign. Cases in point are Torino, Italy with the Slow Food Movement and 2006 Winter Olympics, the Spanish city of Bilbao with its Guggenheim Museum, or Spain's second city of Barcelona with the waterfront development and the 1992 Summer Olympics.

A major difference between the US and Europe, when it comes to place branding, may be that the historical and cultural differences and strong sense of local identity between regions and cities, are more pronounced in Europe. Not that we can see this in most place branding applications, which are generally very superficial as mentioned above. In that sense, place branding practice in most parts of Europe has yet to fulfill its potential in making a significant and lasting contribution to the reputation and competitiveness of places."

South East Asia: Marcus Osborne, destination branding consultant at FusionBrand, in Kuala Lumpur provides a frank assessment of city branding in Asia.

"Singapore and Hong Kong have built internationally respected brands. This was achieved not with creative taglines or cool advertising campaigns, but through their holistic approach to the process of branding. Other Asian cities can benefit by emulating their practices through a better understanding of the concepts and becoming more customer-centered.

Many Asian cities have a top-down focus with a fixation on a tagline and one size fits all communications that try to speak to all, but really speak to none. As an example, in an attempt to boost tourism, the State government of Perak in Malaysia announced that Ipoh would be known as the 'City of White Coffee.' A State executive said, "Ipoh should have its own identity and branding just like Shenzhen (China) that is known as the "Shoe City" and Paris which has long been known as the "City of Fashion." This is an unrealistic expectation and hardly a concept to drive significant tourism growth.

Similarly, the large Indonesian city of Surabaya has branded itself as 'Sparkling Surabaya' to communicate the sparkling of the city as a center for jewelry. The idea was controversial because citizens felt that the concept did not fully represent their city. A more thorough branding process might have helped avoid this situation. On the other hand, the branding of the city of Zamboanga (The Philippines) as 'Asia's Latin City' has gained wide endorsement because it speaks well to the city's culture and strong Latin influence, and appeals to external audiences as well.

The globally accepted principles of place branding are certainly valid in Asia, however the level of their application is very patchy. Few demonstrate what can be considered 'best practice,' and too many are influenced by basic misunderstandings concerning the practice and processes required, and how a city brand should be communicated and perform. In general, too many see city branding as simply a tourism-driven creative advertising campaign or a new slogan."

People's Republic of China: Alastair M. Morrison, Ph.D. CEO at Belle Tourism International Consulting in Beijing provides an interesting perspective on place branding in China.

"It would be fair to say that place branding is in the early stages of development in the People's Republic of China, but the interest in the concept is tremendous. Tourism has been designated as a 'pillar industry' by the national government under the 12th Five-Year Plan and destinations of all sizes are aggressively developing tourism. Government agencies are leading the way in place branding in China, as all the DMOs are run by government.

The major focus is on the domestic Chinese market and thus branding efforts are in the Chinese language and represent the current conditions and cultural norms of the PRC. One of the biggest challenges is in coming up with branding approaches that not only work for the domestic market, but also are effective for international markets. For example, the strategy for Shaoxing: Vintage China for the ancient city in Zhejiang Province has no parallel in the Chinese language or culture.

Generally, place branding in the PRC is not as research-based and sophisticated as in the rest of the world. Most of the place "branding" that takes place is really slogan-making."

Australia: Peter Valerio from Tourism Strategy Development Services in Byron Bay (New South Wales) advises that destination branding was quick to spread from national to state levels in Australia.

"Within a few years of the release of the 'Brand Australia' strategy, branding was well and truly a part of all state tourism organizations' vocabularies. This remains the case, although there is little evidence to suggest that the concept has evolved or developed much. The approach has been very much top-down where the branding of the state-defined tourism regions are an attempt to align with state 'master brands.' A majority of tourism organizations have the term 'brand' in their strategic plans. However, a large gap exists between the inclusion of the term and the existence of a dedicated brand strategy, such as the approach outlined in this book. Where changes have been made, they are typically limited to logos and taglines, and don't always extend to the messages in marketing communications. This is not to say that there aren't some positive, genuine and successful attempts at applying branding strategies such as Flinders Ranges (South Australia), Newcastle (New South Wales/NSW) and Margaret River (Western Australia). In 1998, Wollongong (NSW) became the first regional Australian city to embrace a formalized place branding strategy. It was initiated to address its negative image as an industrial city. The strategy provided the framework to focus many community development initiatives, as well as launch ongoing external communications. In other regions we have seen an increase in the amalgamation of tourism and economic development branding efforts. This approach has been used in the Tweed, Eurobodalla and the Blue Mountains regions (NSW). While the concept of place and destination branding is recognized in Australia, there are a relatively small number of places that are actively or successfully applying it."

CHAPTER TWO

Why Bother with Place Branding?

In the face of increasingly intense competition, ambitious places are objectively evaluating their competitiveness and methods of optimizing their relevance and value to internal and external customers. Many of them are adopting the principles of branding to better manage their identities and how they present themselves in a global marketplace.

Customers are purchasing an intangible when deciding where to visit, relocate, or invest. Consequently, a place's image and reputation are highly influential in these decisions. Joao Freire at Brandia in Lisbon, Portugal agrees, "A place's positive image will attract more people and it will be cheaper for a company wanting to locate there. This is relevant because if the place image is negative the company might have to spend extra money simply to attract the specialized labor it needs to the place. Places that have a negative image will not attract many people and the people attracted will be attracted only because of the compensation packages."

Over time, a successful place brand adds to its own value by generating effectiveness and efficiency in the way that it presents itself. This value is referred to as brand equity, and is its accumulated loyalty, awareness, and financial value. I like to think of it as owning a bank account in the minds of target audiences. Good news, enticing images, and positive experiences are deposits in the bank. But bad news, poor marketing, and sub-standard experiences are like withdrawals from the account. To be strong and resilient, a brand must have sufficient equity on deposit to counter negative occurrences. And bad weather, a natural disaster, scandals or bad experiences do happen, even to good places.

Many city leaders don't understand the benefits and concepts involved in place branding (or marketing for that matter!). Some are simply uncomfortable using the term "branding," or even "marketing," and the city's name in the same sentence. We have found that when city officials think in terms of their city's image or reputation rather than its brand, they are more likely to "get it."

While this is certainly not technically an accurate description of a brand or branding, we have found that it does enable many to better understand and support the concept and its benefits. In an effort to reframe the context for place branding, respected place branding guru Simon Anholt has coined the term, "competitive identity." [5]

The thoughts and associations that come to mind when your city's name is heard or read are likely to have huge financial, political, and social value. Just think for a moment about the number of jobs, businesses, and other organizations that have a stake in its image and reputation. Unfortunately, it is a value that goes largely unrecognized and unappreciated. And perhaps most importantly, unprotected and unmanaged. It rarely gets measured, and never appears on a balance sheet or the job evaluation of a Chamber President, City Manager or Mayor. The level of esteem that a city's name evokes has a direct impact on the health of its tourism, economic development, prestige, and respect. With so much riding on its image, doesn't it make sense to have a plan to cultivate, manage, and protect this most valuable of city assets?

When city officials think in terms of their city's image or reputation rather than its brand, they are more likely to "get it."

While community and civic leaders may debate and procrastinate over the issue of branding, those who actively value their city image soon recognize that developing and managing a brand identity is not an option – it's essential!

What Are the Benefits of Place Branding?

Cities of all sizes often labor over the decision to develop a brand strategy. For small cities it is increasingly becoming a matter of whether they can afford not to embrace the concept if they want to be better organized and be more distinctive and competitive. If the city is allocating funds to marketing programs without consistently clarifying what the city stands for, what it does best, and why it matters to customers, then it is risking (and possibly wasting) public funds. No matter the city's size, a formalized brand strategy can define and manage its competitive identity and channel the energies and resources of partners to orchestrate the best results from their combined investments, however limited.

A place that has a healthy and respected reputation makes it easier to be selected in any competitive setting because the city is seen in a positive light and having qualities and benefits that are good to be associated with. It can be a catalyst for leaders, businesses, and citizens opening doors, being welcomed in the "right circles," gaining seats on the "right" committees, attracting awards and grants, winning bids to host events, and attracting conferences and major events.

Is It Time for a Brand Strategy?

A well-conceived brand strategy can provide increased competitiveness, effectiveness and efficiency in how the city is presented by various city agencies. It sets the guidelines for how the city should be communicated and the delivery of experiences for target audiences.

If individual tactical decisions are driving marketing programs, then it is time for the intervention and strategic discipline of a brand strategy.

If there is a gap between the reality of the city and the expectations and perceptions held by outsiders, then a strategy is needed to bridge this gap. Regardless of whether people hold an overly positive or negative image, the city must address the situation since both of these scenarios can cause problems. An overly positive image can lead to disappointment, while a negative one will lead prospects to spend their time and money elsewhere and possibly perpetuate negative word of mouth.

When individual tactical decisions are driving marketing programs, it's time for the intervention and strategic discipline of a brand strategy to coordinate those disparate activities and make the most of scarce resources. The materials used in your city's marketing portfolio may look great, but without a brand strategy it will be a matter of luck as to whether there is consistency in their look, story, and message. So often the ad of the month syndrome is at play where marketers constantly change their communications in the hope of finding a message that will strike the right chord. Brand planning is the ideal way to avoid this kind of marketing schizophrenia where there is no consistency or clarity to the way the place presents itself. It may be time to develop a brand strategy when you detect one or more of the following conditions:

- The city is not leading with its most distinctive and competitive strengths.
- The need to overcome a dated or inaccurate image.
- New infrastructure developments, revitalization programs or a major event are likely to redefine the place.
- The messages from the city and its partners lack focus, consistency or market relevance.
- There is a gap between the city's promise and its reality.
- Resources are being applied in an inefficient or uncoordinated manner.

It's Not a Magic Wand!

We are living in an era in which some brands like Facebook and iPad, can become enduring household names overnight. On the other hand, some have soared and then crashed just as quickly. Cities are different. Their identities and images have usually been shaped over a very long period, they almost always have small marketing budgets, need to overcome generations of preconceived thoughts and opinions, and must mobilize myriad stakeholders to adopt and use the brand accurately and consistently.

It's difficult to change perceptions and views in the short term. After all, it possibly took decades, maybe even centuries, to form the city's current image. And we know that the "old brain" is much stronger and inflexible than the "new brain" when it comes to replacing old images and stereotypes. For instance, we know of many post-industrial cities whose smoke stack industries closed decades ago, yet those cities are still regarded by some as grimy industrial cities. Similarly, if a city wants to reposition or reinvent itself to be known for something different to the past, outsiders won't catch on to this overnight without extensive and sustained publicity.

Big budgets and better communications alone will not turn around the city's image if its reality is standing in the way. It could be unattractive public spaces, crime, outdated infrastructure or lack of cooperation between businesses that is holding the place back. Today, place branding can engage urban planners, architects and placemaking specialists as readily as tourism and economic development marketers.

Branding can, and does, bring short-term benefits but the true value is long-term and cumulative. Successful place branding is achieved with many small victories, again and again. A city's image is the result of thousands of influences and influencers over an extended period. On the other hand, a Grand Slam approach to branding a place on the basis of one big ad campaign is a sure fire way to blow the budget with little long-term impact. True success will only come from the consistency of messages and outstanding experiences from many sources hitting their mark again, and again, and again.

The benefits of city branding are considerable, however they will not materialize overnight because it will take time for the brand to gain traction within the community, among key partners and with key markets. From the outset, you must be sure that the objectives are clear and realistic, programs are well funded and that there is an understanding of what branding is and isn't. This includes ensuring that no one expects a magic wand. And when the brand strategy is finally revealed, that's when the hard work really begins!

Why Bother with Branding in Tough Times?

The global recession and its recovery are a bumpy ride for places as well as businesses. There's a delicate balancing act to maintain performance levels while adapting to the new behavior of consumers AND reconciling the expectations of political leaders and commercial partners.

When confronted by tough economic times, there is often a knee-jerk reaction by city leaders to cut budgets and demand changes. But change to what? In tough times, what should you cut? What if you cut the wrong things – and make it worse? What if you cut those things that leverage your economic strength and ability to recover? What if you seriously lose market share and it takes decades to recover? How can you be sure to cut the fat and not just corners? The potentially serious implications include losing visitor-generated tax revenues that are important to city budgets.

Just as many corporations and businesses have been in a recession-induced period of Darwinian marketing where weaker competitors cut budgets and lose traction while the smart, determined ones invest and grow, there is a similar clarion call for city leaders. Tough times present an even greater urgency to unify and rally partners, and to focus resources, behavior and decision-making around those competitive strengths that make the city as distinctive, compelling and valued as possible. This is the ideal time to strengthen, adapt, or change strategies to weather these times of uncertainty. In other words – develop a brand strategy! History reveals that when cities sustain or increase their brand investments and marketing during a recession, at a time when competitors are cutting back, they are more likely to improve their market share and marketing performance. Integral to this is the need to invest in innovative product development and improving the sense of place.

Derrick Daye, Global Brand Consultant with The Blake Project notes, "As competing brands pull back, smart community leaders invest and capitalize on the opening to position their municipality as the one of brighter futures. Over the years, hundreds of studies have been conducted that prove those brands that continue to invest in brand building during downturns have more momentum coming out of the downturns than those who don't. Furthermore the advantage they gained is maintained years after."

Kari Westlund, President & CEO of Travel Lane County OR sums it up well, "Our brand strategy has enabled us to create a rallying point to focus the marketing resources, messages and experience delivery of our local stakeholders. During this long recession, this is enabling a level of collaboration and returns on our marketing that may not be possible otherwise."

John Cooper, President of Yakima Valley Convention & Visitors Bureau WA observes, "The truth be told, in the long term a city's brand should transcend economic forces. The brand is shaped in good times and bad based on the experiences and perceptions one associates with the place. I think the key for destination marketers is to continually shape and influence positive perceptions and experiences. Cities with brand strategies that focus on that will be in better shape to weather and recover from the storm."

It's interesting to note New York City's history of proactivity in improving its reputation and image during tough times. The New York Convention & Visitors Bureau was formed in 1934 during the depths of the Great Depression. Then, in the 1970s when just about everyone had written the city off because of deteriorating infrastructure, crime, and financial problems, the state's iconic *I Love New York* campaign was born. Over the next decade and beyond it played an important role in the city's renaissance and was the catalyst for significant growth in the city's visitor economy, as well as in boosting investment and its attractiveness and celebrity.

Unfortunately, for every New York there are hundreds of cities of all sizes that don't recover from their setbacks. Too many walk the tightrope between life and oblivion, hoping for rescue by divine intervention. Ambitious places are becoming increasingly conscious of the need to proactively shape and influence what the world thinks of them and to position and present with strategic intent. A more recent example is Oshkosh WI which launched its brand strategy in 2010 in the depths of the recession and increased its market share, gained an 4% jump in hotel occupancy and event attendance increased by 22% during the first year, and they secured two major new events.

Motivated cities must overcome the temptation to put their strategy on the shelf because of tough times. Instead, they need to use their brand strategy as the focal point to unite local partners and lead the city's economic recovery.

CHAPTER THREE

The Challenges of Branding Places

Hey! Look at Us!

Places of all sizes are being forced to re-examine how they fit into the world and how they can compete to generate economic growth and social well-being for their citizens. Many are making the difficult adjustment from an industrial society into a service and information society. According to urban theorist Richard Florida, "They are increasingly competing for visitors, talent, innovation and creativity. Our world is very spiky where a few successful city regions dominate. A relatively small number of city regions are also home to the greatest numbers of visitors, and the most innovations and inventions which are the result of attracting talent and investment." [6] It's not easy for small cities to attract positive attention, but it ***is*** easy to forget that the rest of the world is not as interested in our hometown as those of us who live there. Today, more than ever, city leaders must maintain an outward perspective and competitive mindset, while balancing local issues.

Each year, thousands of small places across the USA and around the world come to the forefront in the national media for a few minutes in news reports or other events, and then disappear from our radar again. We usually don't spend much time thinking about places other than those that are regularly covered in the media or those where we live, do business in, where friends and relatives live, or we've visited or are planning to visit. When we do hear of them, it is often for the wrong reasons such as bad weather, disasters, crime, accidents, or sometimes in a more positive vein, for major events, famous people, or travelogues. Additionally, the media often unknowingly reinforces negative stereotypes or conveys inaccurate and outdated information about them.

Countering unproductive stereotypes is more of a challenge for cities that have not actively projected a contemporary image or have not had a flow of visitors to see the reality of what the place is really like. Inaccurate images frequently prove to be slow and difficult to eradicate, even in the minds of residents who don't recognize the positive changes occurring around them.

Branding Cities Calls for a Different Approach

The path to revealing a place brand usually involves a multitude of stakeholders and departs from that generally followed for branding corporate products and services. One reason for the variation is the composite nature of places which are a compilation of many independent and competing businesses, products, and experiences that are owned and managed by many different organizations with no single management team or custodian.

When discussing the differences in branding places and consumer products with friends in advertising agencies, they frequently maintain that there is no difference between the two. To some extent they are correct. However there are differences that have a profound influence on the process. These relate to the complexities of ownership, consultation, decision-making, and product development.

A city has many faces and identities. For instance, it may be known as a destination for medical services, golf, education and shopping as well as being home for residents, each with different levels of political, financial and community support.

While a corporate brand may need approval by a marketing team or Board, a city brand usually requires endorsement by several public organizations in which the players may never see completely eye-to-eye. Another problem for many city brands is that important leaders frequently do not have strong marketing or branding credentials, nor do they have a customer-focused perspective. Yet they can exert considerable influence over the process and end result. This is stressed by authors Nigel Morgan and Annette Pritchard who point out, "If a city brand is to be developed as a coherent entity, participants in the process must be aware of the potentially destructive role of politics." [7] The city brand must overcome enmity and rise above politics. Support from political leaders is vital and their understanding must be nurtured because they may not readily recognize the direct relationship between decisions they make and the reputation and attractiveness of the city.

A city brand must be able to stand the test of time, public debate, political scrutiny, media questions, and the analysis of marketing partners.

Community-based brands must withstand a level of public debate that consumer brands rarely endure. A city brand must stand the test of time, public debate, political scrutiny, media questions, and the analysis of marketing partners. The best way to insulate the brand from this scrutiny is to generate buy-in and involvement through an open consultative process.

Vigilant project leaders are necessary to ensure that the process follows an unbiased and objective view while constantly balancing the need to resonate with external customers and optimize support from residents and key stakeholders. There is also the challenge of balancing the influence of particular interest groups. The recommended brand focus might result in certain businesses being a central element, but this determination should be reached without political influence or coercion. Allowing the greatest strengths to rise to the top without undue influence will result in a much stronger and sustainable brand.

Place branding usually requires an approach that is more conciliatory and inclusive than that found with most consumer products. For instance, being very specific with the positioning may unintentionally alienate some locals and cause controversy. Conversely, the trick is to avoid diluting the brand to the point where it loses its strongest competitive edge and ends up being seen as weak and irrelevant.

Additionally, unlike a consumer product such as a soft drink, cities are not discrete or independent entities. A city is much more complex and cannot be reformulated or terminated if it is not popular or is under-performing. Even the prospect of changing the name of the city can prove difficult.

Project leaders who are aware of the differences between the branding of places and consumer goods are in a much better position to adapt to these situations when they become evident. Their presence should not represent a barrier, but a need for further fine-tuning – and a lot of patience!

Is It an Image Problem or Reality?

The terms image and identity are often confused. Brand image relates to how the brand is perceived from the customer's point of view, while brand identity is the unique set of visual, auditory and other stimuli that express the brand and shape its image. Each must be deeply rooted in the foundations of the brand. Think of brand identity as being like the identity of a friend, comprised of his or her name, appearance, personality, speech, ethnicity, and behavior among many other elements. Image, on the other hand, comes from the external view and in this context relates to what people may think of your friend. It is their perceptions, and therefore their reality, of who this person is and what they represent.

Cities often have a reality problem that city leaders prefer not to recognize.

Sometimes we hear that a city has an "image problem." Actually, they often have a "reality problem" that city leaders prefer not to recognize. The real issue is that their image does not match the way they would like to be perceived. Sooner or later the underlying reasons must be addressed.

Strong brands are built on trust. There must be alignment between what the city's brand promises and the reality of the actual experience. If the two are out of sync the brand will not be sustainable unless there are plans – and resources – to bridge the gap. For instance, the New York Times observes that places like Newark, Trenton and even parts of Jersey City (New Jersey) carry the weight of reputations that soured long ago and never recovered. Through times of boom and bust and housing market highs and lows, and even "as developers began seeing potential in urban locales as commuter hubs, the rap on such cities as less than desirable places to live defied erasure, like graffiti in a hard-to-reach spot." [8]

A city has a real image challenge when people outside of it do not accurately know the reality of the place. The imbalance between the internal identity and the external image of many places limits their development. This often happens when the city is projecting itself as one thing, but the reality is much different. For example, the city promotes itself as a place for romantic beach getaways, but visitors find poor restaurant service, substandard hotels, and after-hour beach walkways that are hard to find or poorly lit. Strong, successful brands don't display this kind of dissonance. Place managers must constantly monitor customer satisfaction and "test drive" the services and experiences in their own backyard to ensure that they are of a high standard and are aligned with the promises that they are making.

Kerrie Walters, Executive Director of Grants Pass OR Visitors and Convention Bureau, put it well when she said, "Branding a small community involves many balancing acts. For example, the brand has to match-up with its self-image, yet not be limited by it. It needs to be shaped by its strengths, while stretching them, without becoming contrived and losing its authenticity. What we project to outside audiences must be true to the reality of who and what we are. This has been our mantra in making the Grants Pass brand sustainable."

CHAPTER FOUR

What Is Being Branded and Why?

Are you striving for an overarching place brand for all marketing efforts on behalf of the city? Is it your primary objective to stimulate tourism, relocation and investment, or simply foster community pride? Or is it about the way the city presents itself? What are the geographic boundaries? Is it just the downtown, or the entire city or region? Or is it a thematic brand for special interest markets? There is a fine balance in the geographical, partnership, purpose and political scope of a city brand.

Everyone should be clear about the parameters of the assignment so that you are solving the right problem and not ignoring the underlying issues. Without this clarity, the exercise can quickly descend into confusion, ambiguity and controversy. Some so-called branding efforts result in nothing more than exercises in designing a new look or a feel good tagline.

What Type of Place Brand Are You Developing?

The type of place brand you are looking to define might be very apparent from the start. Is it a destination, investment, community or an overarching place brand? While there may be strong reasons for creating an overarching place brand, it is not always possible to define a single brand platform that is sufficiently potent to meet the diverse audience needs of the city's entire marketing portfolio. It can be done, but you must avoid a one-size-fits-all approach which is based on a series of compromises and moves the focus off customer hot buttons and onto points of commonality that are not distinctive, meaningful or compelling to *any* customers. It needs to be modified

A successful place brand requires a distinctive brand essence or DNA on which the positioning and brand platform can be based.

for each audience. In some cases politics and turf protection work against efforts to develop a competitive and viable brand strategy.

A successful place brand requires a distinctive brand essence or DNA on which the positioning and brand platform can be based. This allows various "sub-brands" to be customized for tourism, investment etc. sharing this DNA, and fine-tuned for their specific audiences. When places reach for less potent propositions on which to base the brand, simply to create "something we can all use," they are on their way to creating an anemic brand. This leads to diluted positioning based on very weak and irrelevant points of difference such as friendliness, quality of life, or community pride. Worse yet, political leaders may dictate that a dominant industry should define the brand. This arbitrary action could possibly render the brand unusable for tourism and others in the marketing portfolio.

Some locations choose to lead with the tourism brand because it projects the lifestyle of the place and this may be central to their economic development strategy. It depends on the objectives, local politics and scale of the city's non-tourism marketing efforts. Additionally, the larger the community, the more difficult the task of defining and gaining consensus for a sustainable overarching brand that will be adopted by all of the city's place marketing agencies.

Shelly Green, president of Durham Convention and Visitors Bureau, highlights how an overarching place brand calls for firm leadership and special care. She says, "The Durham NC brand, based on innovation and creativity, was quickly embraced and activated by groups across the community as diverse as our tourism partners, universities, neighborhoods and dance companies because in the process of distilling it accurately, we identified elements which both external and internal stakeholders valued highly. We were able to strike the right balance because it has come to life across the community and is resonating positively with our key audiences."

Thorough research and consultation enabled Durham to gain community support and enthusiasm for the brand. The primary tagline for Durham, *Where great things happen*™, was designed to encourage diverse community agencies to adapt it in ways to better connect with their particular constituents. For example, with prior approval, partners can substitute other words for the word "*things*" in the tagline to reflect specific Durham strengths. Variations might include *Where great dance happens* or *Where great education happens* or *Where great discoveries happen.* Durham-based Research Triangle Park dovetailed its new brand and tagline perfectly by adopting the line, *The future of great ideas.* The result has been strong alignment and support with more than six hundred local organizations actively deploying the Durham brand in some form.

At times, there may be the need for some fine-tuning even within the tourism brand itself. The Orlando/Orange County Convention & Visitors Bureau found this when their research indicated the need to position the city differently for the meetings market than for the leisure market. Orlando's strong image had been shaped by its outstanding theme parks such as Disney World, Universal Studios, Wet 'n Wild, and SeaWorld. However, research indicated that their positioning for the meetings market needed a more sophisticated identity portraying Orlando as a more "grown up" city offering high-end adult and business-oriented amenities. [9]

In many cases, tourism is the most visible marketing effort on behalf of a city or region. The quality and scope of this effort usually has a strong influence in shaping the city's image. When developing their brand strategies, Grants Pass OR and Santa Rosa County FL each agreed that among their best small business relocation candidates were people who had previously visited as tourists. Hence, tourism was the prominent element in their brand strategies. They reasoned that once someone has a positive experience in the community as a visitor, they are much more open to the idea of relocating their business or family to the area.

What Are Your Objectives?

Most places are trying to be all things to all people, having made little or no attempt to manage their competitive identity. However, external audiences still have an image of a place and this becomes its default positioning. The brand planning process brings increased focus to all aspects of how the city presents itself. Every time a person interacts with it they derive thoughts and build perceptions about it. A community that does not proactively manage these encounters will be positioned anyway by its customers, competitors, and the media, and probably to its disadvantage. It may well be tagged with attributes and an image that it does not want.

The world in which any brand lives is dynamic. There are many forces that constantly influence its relevance, including customer needs, competitors, and the broad political, economic, technological and social environments. Over the years, these forces can have a profound impact on the presentation, positioning and image of a city. Nothing stays the same: consumer tastes change, streetscapes become dated, quality can wane, and what was once attractive and exciting can become dull and uninteresting. To remain competitive a city may have to alter or replace critical elements of its identity and how it is projected. There may be many reasons or objectives for developing a place brand strategy. The decision may be based on a need to:

- Redefine and strengthen the city's competitive identity.
- Foster a more accurate, contemporary and positive image.
- Provide a unifying and strategically focused decision-making framework to guide how the place presents itself.
- Generate improved results for tourism, investment and recruitment ROI.
- Stimulate pride in the city and a renewed sense of purpose.

On one level, leaders may agree on a primary goal, for example to increase visitation, attract newcomers, maximize investment, win major events, improve the image, or other outcomes. But there are underlying dynamics that affect these performance outcomes and these need to be monitored and managed. Like consumer goods, cities have a lifecycle where their popularity may rise and fall over time, as does the relevance and quality of their offerings. This particularly becomes apparent in regard to their relevance and reputation for specific audiences.

How Will You Achieve Your Objectives?

While the branding of consumer goods might involve the development of the product as result of the brand planning and positioning process, the situation for place branding rarely follows this path. In most circumstances, the place already exists and the capacity to substantially change the place (or its built environment) might vary, and the place brand manager probably doesn't control or own critical elements of it. Additionally, for many cities it's really a matter of bringing clarity and focus to its identity and communications. Most cities have not previously had a formalized brand strategy or any prescribed positioning when they initially consider developing a brand strategy. In most cases their positioning, or lack of it, has evolved organically over time and now influences how people think of it.

The brand managers for consumer goods have a number of options for addressing their product's image, consumer tastes and competitor actions. They can revitalize or reposition it, milk it for revenue, sell it, or kill it off. On the other hand, community leaders and place brand managers have fewer and different options because they certainly can't sell the city or kill it off. Place branding usually involves refreshing the look and feel of the existing brand (even if it has evolved organically) or introducing substantial changes to appeal to new audiences, thus repositioning the place.

You may have noticed that some people confuse rebranding with repositioning, using the terms "rebranding" and "repositioning" interchangeably. One can consider rebranding as the wrapping paper and ribbons on the outside and repositioning as the gift itself. Putting fancier or more colorful decorations on the outside will not change what people think of the gift inside. Repositioning is much deeper and is about ensuring that the gift lives up to the expectations created by the wrapping and ribbons. It might range from minor changes and enhancements at a minimum, to totally reinventing the place in the extreme cases – it could mean a totally new gift. It is important to note that rebranding does play a role in repositioning, but it comes later in the planning process after you have clearly identified the optimal positioning and have decided or introduced the product related changes.

Achieving your objectives will require knowing the current state of the city, where it has opportunities, and the strategic approaches that may be needed to bridge the gap. Consider whether the strategies should involve:

1. Rebranding (or refreshing)
2. Repositioning
3. Reinventing
4. Doing nothing and maintaining the status quo (and possibly the downward spiral)

1. Rebranding: Change the Wrapping

Rebranding involves a process where an outdated or irrelevant brand identity is modified and re-launched with a new focus. In the context of places the term "refresh" might be more appropriate. It's sort of like a facelift and for consumer goods may include a name change, new logo and colors, updated packaging, point of sale material, a new advertising campaign. For a place, this might extend to improving streetscapes, cleanliness, signage and service delivery to ensure they are relevant to the brand and contemporary needs and tastes.

The common mantra for rebranding is: "Do no harm!" You must be sure that the brand platform is not disturbed because rebranding involves the same audiences, the same offering and basically the same positioning. The actions should not risk diminishing the brand equity that has been earned over time.

Rebranding is fine-tuning the way in which products and experiences continue to be presented to the same markets, with minor changes.

Rebranding is fine-tuning the way in which products and experiences continue to be presented to the same markets, with minor changes. In rebranding it's mainly the look and feel – the identity – that is receiving attention. If the analysis in Step Two (Chapter Nine) shows the current positioning to no longer be relevant, then simple rebranding in the form of new wrapping paper will not be sufficient to address the situation.

Even long established destinations need to periodically refresh to sustain their popularity and relevance. Waikiki, in addition to being Hawaii's most visited destination, has also been out of sync with visitor perceptions of the 'idyllic Hawaiian vacation.' Hawaii Visitors & Convention Bureau research revealed that Waikiki should convey a more modern and evolving interpretation of the spirit of Aloha – a beachfront melting pot in which Western and Polynesian cultures combine to create the 'Waikiki Phenomenon.' The objective was to show that the experience of Aloha isn't locked in the past, but rather a living, unique culture and lifestyle that can be experienced in Waikiki. The change is reflected in upgraded streetscapes, marketplaces and the beachfront.

Newcastle, Australia (my home town) is attempting to shed its long established 'Steel City' image with a colorful rebranding program. This includes a new logo and tagline (*See Change*) as well as increased promotions through tourism websites, brochures and signage. The city has also installed sixteen visitor information kiosks throughout the city. "This rebranding will enable us to consistently promote a more contemporary view of the city – a genuine, ever-changing, vibrant and energetic place that is home to hardworking people and world-class industries," the City's Tourism and Economic Development Manager, Simon McArthur said.

Essex (England) is rebranding its 350 mile shoreline as the *Discovery Coast*, which they hope will give the coastline a new sense of identity and promote it as a more versatile destination. Elli Constantatou, from Visit Essex, said, "We want to lay claim to this title because the shores of Essex have so many unique features, which both residents and those outside the county just aren't aware of." [10]

2. Repositioning: Change the Way They See Us

After conducting a competitive positioning analysis, the city may find it necessary to completely change people's attitudes and perceptions toward the place relative to competitors. This calls for the city to address the tough issues that may be adversely impacting perceptions and behavior toward the place. Repositioning involves the efforts to turn the page on these issues. It could mean a substantial change to the features, benefits and experiences relative to competitors, or targeting new audiences, or both. In order to achieve successful repositioning, it's preferable to make careful, incremental refinements rather than attempt to take the potentially risky and expensive step to new positioning in one move.

Repositioning may become a priority when a city finds itself with significant new infrastructure, hallmark events, or cultural investments that represent major changes. A gap may form between its old (and current) image and its new reality if the changes are not conveying to external markets. Repositioning may also be necessary when a city decides that it's time to correct long-held negative images. Specific changes such as new infrastructure, crime reduction, innovative urban design and major events may be important stimulants for changing the way that people think about the place, relative to other options.

A gap may form between its old (and current) image and its new reality if the changes are not conveying to external markets.

Repositioning a city and changing what it stands for in the customer's mind can be a challenging and expensive proposition. It takes much more than a great advertising campaign. Las Vegas learned this in the early 1990s when it attempted to reposition the city as a place for family entertainment. This involved resort, hotel, attraction and other infrastructure. After several years, they recognized that this strategy was not providing the desired results and so repositioned the city for adult freedom, thus setting in place a whole new vision for developments and entertainment.

Changing perceptions can be a long-term proposition. Even then, there is no guarantee of success. It can be made even more difficult, as Las Vegas discovered, when the city must balance the tasks of changing its identity and attracting new markets all while retaining current customers. Las Vegas was able to successfully recapture its prized position in large part through dramatic infrastructure developments, exciting new entertainment, innovative hospitality and its award-winning *What happens here, stays here*™ campaign. In a similar effort, on the East Coast, the state of New Jersey has initiated an ambitious strategy to revitalize and reposition Atlantic City as an urban, beachside leisure center and more than just a tired gaming destination.

The outstanding art glass of famed artist Dale Chihuly was one of the inspirations for Tacoma WA to shed its industrial image and reposition itself based on being a center for world-class art glass. Developed two years before the city opened two new major art museums, the CVB and the City took the opportunity to mobilize stakeholders and commence the local advocacy and marketing communications to reposition the place. Of course, in cases like this care must be taken to ensure that the city does not make promises it can't keep, or claim a position that it isn't going to reach within a reasonable period of time. Tacoma successfully bridged this gap to reposition itself and is now amazing visitors with the transformation that has taken place.

In the late 1970s the small city of Chemainus on Victoria Island (B.C. Canada) was facing exceptionally difficult times due to major declines in its timber and mining industries. Some thought the town was finished. A revitalization program to encourage tourism was introduced based on transforming the city into an outdoor art gallery featuring murals on many of its buildings. Beginning in 1982 and continuing still today, 41 murals have been commissioned, most of them portraying the history of the city. The outdoor gallery has encouraged many businesses, including a live professional theatre, antique dealers, and restaurants to invest in the community. Chemainus is now a popular tourist destination and is regarded as one of the world's preeminent mural cities.

The Israeli city of Eilat located on the northern tip of the Red Sea, is repositioning to be seen as a city of diverse attractions and shopping, and not simply a resort and port. The objective is to become known as the only Western tourism city on the Red Sea. In addition to new marketing communications, it will involve upgrading the promenade and public beaches and development of a central park.

3. Reinventing: Take a Second Lease on Life

This could be considered as positioning on a grand scale. The reinvention of a place is a planned transformation that may take the form of new infrastructure, major events, a new theme, or possibly urban regeneration with dramatic new public, retail and residential developments. It totally transforms the character of the place, and often its economic base. This radical departure from the past directly impacts the city's image and character.

Visionary city leaders may decide to stimulate major private and public infrastructure projects to completely redefine the place. These projects rarely have the principles of formalized city branding in mind when they are initiated. It is often a case where the branding process must play catch-up with the city leaders, investors, developers, and urban planners, and realign or reposition outdated external images of the city with the new reality of the place as it is emerging.

Strategies to reinvent a city, neighborhood or district are expensive. A large financial commitment is necessary to inject new life into the area to attract visitors, residents, conference delegates, students, or investors. In these situations the "brand team" is just as likely to be a team of architects and developers who may be solely focused on their developments and not on branding. But increasingly, urban designers and architects are adopting the principles of place branding.

Malcolm Allan of Colliers International agrees, adding, "Traditional town planning can only benefit, in my view, from a strategic and practical alliance with place branding. It enables places to be created that meet the needs of identified audiences. We need places that provide much more satisfying and well thought through experiences that are inspired by the city's brand, and the agreed purpose and values of the place."

Cities are revitalizing their downtowns as cultural, sporting, harborside and entertainment districts, and in the process are redefining the way that people think of the whole city. These major redevelopment projects may occur over a long period such as those involving East Village Calgary in Alberta Canada, Portland's Pearl District, and Baltimore Harbor in Baltimore MD. The downtown redevelopments in Corpus Christi TX, Wembley City (England), and the Renaissance Project in Chester (England) were all initiated to transform their city images. They are not only aiming to attract more visitors, but to specifically transform the interest of residents in the entertainment and recreational values of their communities.

Addressing its dated industrial image, Holon (Israel) adopted its brand vision in 1995 to turn the city into a 'children's city' with a focus on culture and education for children and families. The city set in place a visionary process of investment and innovation which included the addition of the only children's museum in Israel, story gardens combining the worlds of literature, art and leisure, numerous high profile festivals, science and art enrichment centers for preschoolers, and more to come. These investments were accompanied by a restructuring of the education system, urban design improvements and plans to influence change through housing, transport, public spaces and zoning. The end result is a total transformation of the city.

Another dramatic example of a city reinventing itself is Leavenworth WA. In 1965, business owners made the decision to adopt a Bavarian theme and commence remodeling the entire town. While Leavenworth has successfully redefined itself, it is not a transformation that pleases everyone. Some cite it as lacking authenticity, being too contrived, and even turning the city into a theme park. This highlights the importance of community consultation to ensure that ideas for redevelopment are closely aligned with the community's vision and values. Although Leavenworth has its critics, it seems to have been a formula that has worked for most residents and its target audiences.

CHAPTER FIVE

Prepare to Start: Mobilize the Forces

Like an athlete preparing to compete in a major event, you must complete careful and detailed preparation before getting to the starting line. Let's look at some of the preliminary actions needed to prepare a sound foundation that will generate the support, understanding and endorsement of the branding project. A city may have distinctive natural and cultural attributes that mark it as a special place. However, without strong and effective leadership and genuine collaboration it will never reach its optimum strength as a brand. It takes the right people investing time, expertise, knowledge, finances and the long-term power and commitment of their office to build an influential place brand.

Planning for Community-Based Brands

By adopting the principles of branding, you are introducing a more strategically focused approach to how your city is presented. Branding should provide the strategic and decision-making framework and toolkit to better orchestrate the messages and experiences emanating from the city. It should be strategic (not tactical) and approached with a long-term view.

The overall process for formulating a city's brand strategy is much the same irrespective of its size. However, individual elements and emphasis will vary according to the available budget, stage of development, market sophistication, complexity of its economic base, and the accuracy of its existing image in key markets. Each place brings its own dynamics which is displayed in its products, politics, history, attitudes and performance.

Economic development and destination marketing organizations are usually the best situated entities to plan, coordinate, and manage the branding process. They generally have strong relationships with a wide cross-section of other organizations and are the most committed to the marketing of the city. Their mandate and their externally-focused constituents have a strong, direct influence on the overall image and marketing activities. In other cases, the project manager may be the city administration, particularly if developing an overarching place brand. In these situations, the mayor or city manager's office may be in the best position to lead the effort, especially if they embrace the need to nurture and protect the city's image. Interestingly, organizations in Britain have been created to specifically develop and implement a brand strategy for a city or region. They have full-time staff and in most cases have a mandate to manage the overarching place brand. These organizations include Southampton Connect, Marketing Edinburgh Ltd., and CreativeSheffield.

One thing is for sure: there is no "silver bullet" or one-size-fits-all solution that will quickly deliver a sustainable brand. Decades of working with countries, cities and regions has led us to create our highly successful *7A Destination Branding Process*. It can be applied to all forms of place branding. The *7A Process* had its genesis during my years of international branding for Australia and other countries, and later evolved through tourism marketing and strategic planning assignments for communities in Australia and North America. This led me to formulate an approach that is a blend of community planning disciplines, the research and analytical techniques used in destination development, and the strong integrated tourism marketing and brand planning principles learned from working with some of the world's leading destinations.

As the name implies, the *7A Destination Branding Process* leads cities through seven steps that encourage thoroughness and ensures that important actions are not overlooked or minimized. It often proves to be a game-changer that revolutionizes and refocuses the place's strategic intent, stimulates unity and relationships, and improves the impact of marketing programs. It is also applicable to overarching place brands and economic development brands.

It Must Be the CEO's Baby

The president, executive director, or CEO of the lead organization must be actively engaged in every aspect of the brand planning and development, and breathe vitality into the assignment. We have found that the only way for the brand to take off is having a CEO who "gets it" and has the passion, authority, skills and vision to make it work. If he or she takes a passive role, the brand will almost certainly fail.

Understandably, there may be many legitimate distractions that consume the CEO's time. However, the brand is at the heart of every activity directed toward how the place will present itself for years to come, so it is worth every minute that he or she can devote to it. While the CEO may want to delegate aspects of the day-to-day management of the process to others, he must remain intimately involved in crafting and managing the strategy. This visible engagement by the CEO will ensure that he or she:

- Makes a strong statement to everyone that this is important.
- Fully understands and takes an active role in shaping the strategic rationale of the brand.
- Can present the brand with authority and enthusiasm.
- Ensures that the brand thrives throughout the organization and at critical touchpoints with customers.
- Strengthens their personal relationship, and that of the lead organization, with key constituents.
- Leads the educative role in furthering the understanding of the brand.
- Champions the brand's long term viability and funding.

Place Brands Don't Belong to the Marketing Department

Branding is often mistakenly regarded as just another word for marketing or advertising, and belonging to the marketing department. In fact, it needs to be far more pervasive. The brand should first and foremost be regarded as part of a strategic toolkit and as the central organizing and decision-making principle guiding the way the city exhibits itself. This makes it everyone's job to a greater or lesser extent!

While a strong brand has many benefits for customers (including making their buying decisions much easier), it should also make internal decision making clearer for the leaders, staff, marketers, vendors, and stakeholders because all actions are filtered according to their likely impact on the brand. At the heart of a true city brand is a unifying movement that results in hundreds and sometimes thousands of actions coming into alignment at critical moments.

A genuine mandate for branding success may require a change of mindset within, and between, many organizations.

If the management and advocacy for the brand is confined to the folks in the tourism marketing department, it's unlikely to reach the expected level of potency. When leaders get past the notion that a brand relates only to marketing or advertising they may be more willing to remove impediments and introduce the type of thinking, resources and cooperation that will empower brand building and challenge the community to achieve its greatest potential.

Brand Management Often Involves Change Management

After decades of place branding assignments, I recognize that they are fundamentally an exercise in change management. A successful city brand often requires changes to regulations, laws, systems, budgets, processes, resources, and recruitment. Above all, it may call for a change of attitudes and relationships. The first casualty may be the old "that's the way we've always done it" attitude. For many people, the prospect of new focus, concepts, priorities, and partnerships causes extreme resistance. It removes them from their comfort zone and challenges entrenched attitudes. In these situations you need to expose them to the benefits that can come from the alternative approaches so they can gain the confidence and trust in the project and its outcomes.

A genuine mandate for branding success may require a change of mindset within, and between, many organizations. It may involve the need to overcome individual disagreements and turf protection. Tearing down unhelpful barriers, attitudes, and processes are major steps forward. Collaboration, networking, and integration are the signatures of a healthy brand. This certainly takes more than the efforts of the tourism or marketing offices alone. It can engage the people responsible for urban planning, parking, signage, parks, education and business licensing. Some of these people may have no idea of their daily impact on the identity of their city.

Take the Lead

One of the unexpected benefits of the collaborative approach is that it provides an unprecedented opportunity for the lead organization to showcase its role as a community and industry leader. Time and again, we have seen the process become the rallying point to re-energize the lead organization, its constituents and the marketing of their city. The challenge is to sustain this heightened enthusiasm and use it as a catalyst to consolidate the organization's position as one of the city's most valuable leadership organizations. It is an ideal time to move people beyond turf building, internal politics and the dated opinions that may have prevailed in the past.

We have noticed that the process tends to gain added credibility and support when the DMO reaches outside of "the usual suspects" and canvasses the views of a wider range of constituents.

Lead organizations rarely have a better opportunity to display their value than through this process. We have discovered that the process tends to gain credibility and support when there is a genuine effort to reach beyond "the usual suspects" and canvass the views of a wider range of constituents.

This was the experience of Anne Jenkins at Travel Medford (Oregon) who said, "The consultative planning process we used generated incredible buy-in among our Board members, partners and stakeholders. It established us as a community leader and contributed directly toward a better understanding and working relationship in what we do for the city and region. We were able to make changes that probably would not have been possible for years had we not used external assistance, engaged city leaders and developed a strategy that has been built on collaboration and thorough research."

The progress and outcomes first from the planning, and then the launch and implementation are greatly improved when participants are knowledgeable about place brands and branding. We have found that offering educational seminars, webinars, briefings and books like this to those who will be actively involved in the process creates not only a more rewarding experience for them, but support and confidence in the long-term. Many also take the newly acquired knowledge back to their own businesses and apply it there.

Great Leaders Lead to Great Brands

Cities are alive with myriad agendas, visions, objectives and egos – all in play at the same time. Most cities have multiple centers of influence and while many individuals and organizations are very customer, business, and future-oriented, some may be firmly locked in the past and fearful of any changes. Others are less concerned about economic benefits as they are about the social and environmental impacts that promoting the community will bring. Still others question why money is being spent on branding, placemaking and marketing when there are other civic needs.

Communicating the benefits of place branding to local citizens and organizations will help in winning support and boosting community pride.

Great brands are more likely to emerge when leaders step out of their comfort zone and show creativity, vision and courage. This is a powerful signal to observers and may stimulate 'out of the box' ideas and collaboration among some of the most unlikely of partners. Brands will achieve their greatest potential when there is passion, courage, and a strong commitment by the leadership of the city. Success takes much more than lip service. While local opinions are very important, it is vital for leaders to understand that the views of their external customers should be the final arbiters on what will define the city's most competitive brand.

Place branding is a team sport, best played with people of all ages and interests.

This project must not only be **seen** as a partnership between government, business and non-profits – it must actually **be** one! If it is dominated by government officials and their staff it will almost certainly fail to gain traction. City council members often do not have the breadth of experience, perspective, and credibility to critique the technicalities of the brand in detail or to objectively generate the cross-city enthusiasm and partnerships needed for success. The other guaranteed formula for an unhealthy brand is one where the city council appoints the brand committee comprised of people who have passed their political or friends test. Place branding is a team sport, best played with people of all ages and interests with a healthy dose of what's best for the common good – and with an out of town coach in the form of a qualified place branding specialist.

Roger Brooks, President of Destination Development International suggests, "While the city or municipality can take the lead in terms of funding, all successful brands are, ultimately, founded on grassroots efforts. Branding is about differentiating yourself from everyone else. It's about narrowing your focus not throwing a blanket over everything. Here's the problem with top-down only efforts: elected officials were elected to be all things to all people. Brands can't be! End of story."

The branding and marketing of cities can be complex and sometimes, controversial. In order to avoid or minimize controversy, political and opinion leaders must understand the assignment and embrace the many benefits that the strategy will bring. If they persist in regarding it as a process to deliver a new motto (as they might call it) or logo for the city, the project will achieve less than stellar results. They must understand that this is a strategic assignment to enhance the city's economic well-being and competitiveness. It goes to the core of everything that the city will do when presenting its best face to the world. When they fully grasp and support this, they are not only able to deflect criticism but will become influential brand champions who signal that this project is important to constituents and the future of the city.

At times, achieving the brand vision and delivering the brand promise requires leadership to break from the status quo and exert influence through their office. They may need to call for new resources, new and long-term organizational structures, a review of some city ordinances, beautification programs, and performance reviews. They may even be called on to slaughter a few "sacred cows." As previously stated, in many respects branding is also an exercise in change management and relies very much on healthy relationships, cooperation and a genuine preparedness to adapt to new situations.

Another obstacle to the sustainability of city brands is the turnover in leadership, especially elected officials with term limits. "Often, you'll have political leaders who agree that someone should put the place on the map but then say, 'It's not my job' because they will be out of here in a few years," says Rod Underhill. "There needs to be sufficient conviction among the other civic organizations and leaders that branding can withstand a turnover in leadership, and avoid stop-start marketing," he adds. [11] At this early stage, give consideration to the longevity and sustainability of the project by including people who are not likely to leave the city, elected office or their respected position in the near future.

It takes time, but investing the effort to garner the endorsement and participation of the leading executives, opinion leaders, public officials and the media will directly benefit the long-term viability of the brand. Some of them may not be directly involved in the ongoing brand management, but their decisions and support may have profound leverage and influence. It pays to be prepared for a variety of responses from individuals and organizations. To address their particular views, they should be exposed to the basic concept of branding and its benefits. Customized presentations may be necessary; each designed to ensure that participants understand place branding, the project's objectives, the benefits of greatest interest to them, and importantly, that the project is much more than a feel good exercise. Simply completing the brand strategy, and then presenting it to these important participants is likely to result in a very weak brand or, even worse, controversy.

Brand planning must be based on open exchanges and collaboration to capture the information and insights needed to reveal the most competitive identity possible. This may call for project managers to break down territorial silos that may exist between, and within, key entities. This helps to ensure that there is no gap between what the city promises and the actual experiences that customers will enjoy.

A holistic or 360° approach to place branding requires a break from the age-old way of doing things. Hence, opinion leaders need to be the catalysts and champions for cultural shifts at important points around the city. They should agree to participate in a dialogue that corrects any misunderstandings about the project and provide their unambiguous and hearty public endorsement. There is also the need for managing the expectations in regard to what the project is, and isn't. From the outset, you must ensure that the project budget isn't associated with only a new logo and tagline. Otherwise, from the start you will be defending against accusations that you are spending the entire budget on a logo, when it is actually a small part of the budget. Be aware that misinformation like this can seriously derail the project.

Give Them a Voice, Then Listen!

Canvassing the opinions of stakeholders can reveal great ideas and perspectives, and can provide important clues as to where the "land mines" or likely trouble spots may be later in the process. Importantly, consultation is extremely valuable in clearing the way to reveal the brand. Within the community there are residents, businesses, and political and opinion leaders who will have comments, knowledge, and perspectives that should be considered. After they are identified, the level and nature of their involvement in the project can be determined.

Brad Dean, President and CEO of Myrtle Beach Area Chamber of Commerce, has some excellent advice for those starting a brand planning process for their city. Brad says, "The brand effort does not belong behind closed doors, in an ivory tower or within the boardroom. Involve everyone – the stakeholders, the web programmer, the mayor, the media – involve anyone and everyone who has a reason to care. Involve your mother-in-law if you have to. Just make certain that anyone who has a vested interest gets a chance to be involved. I believe places that haven't done this have introduced the new brand to a chorus of boos and jeers, with community stakeholders often announcing their disdain for the new ideas. Making sure to involve key people in the initial brainstorming and branding process is definitely something that's important to consider."

The task of uniting people with diverse political, cultural and social interests like those found in Santa Monica CA would seem like an impossible task. But according to Misti Kerns, CEO of the Santa Monica Convention & Visitors Bureau, "When you can bring together 11 different interest committees, from the right and the left, and have everyone agreeing on a single item, then I'd have to say that's success, and that's what our branding has done for our community."

Opportunities to participate may include participation in the Brand Advisory Committee, face-to-face interviews, workshops, an invitation to complete a survey, or periodic briefings. Don't hesitate to invite critics and or those who may be cynical about such projects, as they may change their opinions or gain greater respect for your efforts and provide support in other ways.

Select Your Brand Advisory Committee

A small Brand Advisory Committee representing a cross section of community and business organizations should be assembled to oversee the brand planning process. Their primary responsibility is to recommend approval and adoption of the brand strategy. Members should be carefully selected and only appointed after a list of prospective candidates has been thoroughly evaluated. The Committee should ideally comprise 8-12 representatives. Although there is no "correct" number, the fewer the better! The more people on the Committee, the higher the risk that too many disparate opinions, unrelated issues and politics will start to play a role. This can slow things down, impair the sense of cooperation and objectivity that is needed, and dilute the brand itself.

In the mix of backgrounds and experience that will be represented on the committee, it's helpful to invite some who are marketing and brand savvy, others who have a good pulse on the community, another who is politically savvy (and connected), and others who have a perspective of the community competitiveness in the outside world. This mix can lead to a broad spectrum of views, the strategic evaluation of concepts, and ensures that the approach is sensitive to the values and realities of the community.

At least one individual from the organization responsible for the eventual implementation and management of the brand should attend Committee meetings. This helps keep things grounded and builds knowledge about the brand – and fosters a greater sense of ownership. We have found that the best Advisory Committee participants are those who are:

- Objective and participate with an open mind
- Looking beyond their own self interest
- Passionate for getting the best possible result for the city
- Future-focused beyond looking at short-term and tactical
- Well-respected and able to generate acceptance and support when the brand is implemented
- Open to fresh ideas and think "outside the box"
- Supportive, even if the new brand is not directly focused on their organization
- Able to view the city from the customer's perspective

Stakeholders realize that the DMO cannot achieve its objective alone and that they all need to work in an active partnership.

The Advisory Committee's involvement should be integrated throughout the brand planning process, especially at critical milestones. They may not necessarily be authorized to give approval or make major decisions, but they are an invaluable sounding board to provide guidance to the brand specialist and DMO executives. They should be representative of the community and, as a Committee, recommend approval of the final brand strategy to the client Board. This will ensure that solutions do not lose touch with market situations, resources, implementation capabilities, politics, and the self-image and values of the city.

The Committee's involvement should start with an intensive briefing on the relevance of place branding, the planning process, their role, and a discussion to reveal their aspirations for the project. While some participants may be very experienced in marketing and branding, it still pays to provide this briefing. Starting with an informative presentation about branding cities ensures that everyone is on the same page. If participants interpret different meanings for various terms, their objectives and expectations may result in a confused situation and much spinning of your wheels.

Make optimal use of your committee. They shouldn't be arguing for hours whether the logo should be red or green. Deftly manage their responsibilities and guard against becoming bogged down with minutiae. They should be focused on the central organizing thought, its implications, general oversight, and how to generate support when orchestrating the on-brand actions across the city.

It is not unusual for Advisory Committee members to develop a strong sense of ownership and pride in their contribution. Their enthusiasm and commitment is priceless as the project moves forward. Many will eventually step forward to become active champions for the brand because they are so engaged and knowledgeable about all aspects of its creation. Hopefully, they will also realize that the DMO cannot achieve its objectives alone and that they all need to work in an active partnership.

Who Is Your Brand Manager?

A meaningful and sustainable brand will not grow in an ad hoc way. It takes many guiding hands. After being launched, the brand will still need firm, consistent hands to meticulously implement the strategy and encourage partners to perform their parts. If this is to be an overarching brand, the task of ensuring accurate and consistent deployment across all partners can be quite a challenge. The task is only slightly easier for destination brands with a primary focus on tourism.

In addition to the lead organization managing the brand, it requires an individual to nurture, promote, manage, and "police" the brand as it is bought to life across all platforms and partners. This person is the brand's most important friend. He or she is the brand manager and should be involved in the project from its earliest days.

The brand manager must not only lead the efforts inside the lead organization, but also energize the outreach programs and briefings for members, marketing service vendors, and local partners. The manager is the enabler and protector who is responsible for activating the resources, talent, creativity, focus, and consistency to oversee and grow this extremely valuable asset. He or she is responsible for maintaining the integrity of the brand by ensuring that all copy, images, design, messages and experiences conform to the brand strategy.

The brand manager should be a strong communicator, and a marketing-savvy leader with the credibility, experience and vision to successfully guide the brand's implementation. It is common in a small city for the CEO or marketing manager of the DMO to take the role of brand manager. However, a few DMOs have created the full-time position of Brand Manager, and others have created the position only for the first few years of deployment. This person, while having ultimate responsibility, may work closely with the marketing manager and possibly a brand management committee to oversee the brand. These responsibilities should be reflected in their job descriptions and have the endorsement of the Board.

It is important to keep in mind that the brand doesn't belong to any one individual. It is the property of the entire community and its customers. In addition to reviewing internal uses, the brand manager must monitor the many forms of communications and experiences that emanate from the city's other messengers and partners in order to encourage brand alignment, consistency and coherence across all applications.

While the brand manager is the main custodian of the brand, the brand champions may be in various key organizations throughout the city and charged with advancing the brand vision for tourism, economic development, education, and so on. Brand champions are well respected individuals who are able to open doors and rally support for the brand within the community and key markets.

Just as a financial auditor has authority, the brand manager must also be empowered with the authority to do the job. If no-one is specifically designated in this role, the brand strategy implementation might be patchy and stray from the set path. Without a designated brand manager with high level authority and energy, there is the possibility that things may revert back to the "bad old ways," or actually never leave the "bad old ways."

Match Your Goals and Budget

Whether your goal is to attract more visitors, new businesses or students, or to address an unfocused image, you must define your goals and objectives from the outset. Be certain that you have allocated sufficient funds to facilitate the most thorough brand planning process possible. These funds should be sufficient to engage a branding specialist to lead the process. When requesting the budget, it's important to secure additional resources for the launch and initial implementation of the strategy. This one-off allocation will prove to be a smart investment because the brand strategy can then be launched with the greatest impact possible, and without delay.

Questions

- Which is the lead organization?
- What is your internal decision-making and approval process for the project?
- Which organization and individual will be responsible for day to day liaison with the place branding specialist?
- Which organizations must be consulted prior to final sign-off on the strategy?
- Who is the Brand Manager?

CHAPTER SIX

Prepare to Start: Selecting Place Branding Expertise

Once it's been decided to develop a place brand, the city's next critical decision is how to undertake and manage the process. Will it attempt to handle the research, analysis and strategic development internally or will it engage the services of specialists? If the decision is made to engage qualified specialists, the consideration then becomes which firm and under what conditions.

From the outset, stakeholders need to be aware that branding is a strategic management tool and much more than a new logo, catchy tagline or advertising campaign. A true brand strategy is a beacon that guides all aspects of how the city presents itself, unifies stakeholders to deploy the brand, and consistently offers superior experiences. Achieving this requires extensive research, stakeholder consultation, and creative and collaborative thinking. It also calls for a thorough understanding of the nuances of place branding and marketing. Understanding what place branding entails will more effectively guide the way the city approaches the selection of specialist services.

The selection of the company to develop the city's brand will have long term repercussions. Therefore project leaders must first agree on the overall objectives and clarify exactly how they interpret 'branding' (perhaps it's being confused with a marketing plan, logo or an advertising campaign). This will go a long way toward the best use of resources, making difficult decisions, and recruiting the right specialists.

Knowing how to go about the selection process itself is equally important. There are countless firms that claim to have expertise to guide you through place branding, so you need the know-how to clearly assess each firm's specific capabilities and detect those that are most likely to over-promise and under-deliver. In particular, you must be able to evaluate whether the firm truly understands the fundamentals of branding places and has the specific experience and expertise relevant to your initiative.

The observation of Zeitgeist Consulting President Bill Geist is particularly relevant, "There's an ocean of difference between a brand and a slogan. And, yet, we're seeing that body of water crossed with alarming regularity by firms that are jumping on the bandwagon and showering unsuspecting destination marketers with overblown promises of Nike-like brand awareness. Sure, every DMO pro dreams of developing a brand that resonates. But so many of the recent concepts we've seen from some of the 'brand-houses' out there are nothing more than catchy slogans that could be interchanged between places as easily as changing your shirt. Of course, after dropping $80,000 on a brand nobody wants to admit that what they're holding in their hand is a slogan … so the dirty little secret continues to hide under wraps. But it's there all the same: these aren't brands."

Many will claim to be brand experts, but the reality is this: brand strategy is at best a by-product of what they do.

Organizations are often sold a 'branding' service which is actually nothing more than advertising, public relations, or some other communications principle. The reason is that many design firms, pr groups, ad agencies, research houses, architectural firms, and business consultants offer 'branding' services. But they do so in order to sell their core expertise – their graphic design, pr, advertising, research, architecture, and business consulting services. Many will claim to be brand experts, but in reality: brand strategy is at best a by-product of what they do.

It Takes Objectivity and the Right Outside Expertise

One of the greatest challenges for those involved in the process is being objective and customer-focused. This may be the place where participants were born and educated, and locals sometimes have a bias that limits their view of the city from the perspective of an outsider. This highlights the need for outside advice which lends the impartiality and objectivity that is very difficult to get from within the community. Some of the communities we have worked with initially attempted to develop the brand strategy themselves. After struggling with their own internal dynamics, they realized that an outside specialist can succeed where stagnation and disagreement may otherwise limit progress because of entrenched attitudes and a reluctance to cooperate with long-standing opponents.

Engaging outside specialists also allows the city to harness the experience and skills that may not be available locally. A qualified consultant can guide the group through all of the difficult analysis and decisions that may be overlooked or glossed over by locals. Many cities and even their communications agencies have an increasing appreciation for the expertise needed to address the complexities and demands of place branding. We have experienced this when some advertising agencies have wisely recognized that they were not place brand strategists and hired us to develop the brand strategy component for their clients.

The first important consideration is to recognize that the brand strategy and implementation are not the same thing. The project should be divided into two stages: (1) the formulation of the brand strategy, requiring strong research, analytical and strategic skills, as well as a detailed knowledge of tourism, economic development, product development and placemaking, and (2) the strategy implementation, possibly requiring advertising, web design, public relations, and publishing expertise. While some firms will claim to do both, it pays to gain a clear understanding of the depth of their experience. Recruit specialists appropriate to each phase. If your brand planning is thorough, it should shine a light into all areas of your city and its capacity to engage and delight your customers. The firm selected for strategy development must also have the capacity to consider organizational issues, partner relations, tourism and relocation dynamics, product development and investment, as well as placemaking and wayfinding.

Destination Marketing Association International highlights the dilemma that cities face in recruiting the right type of expertise in their publication, *Destination BrandScience* by Duane Knapp. "Qualified, skilled brand expertise in strategic development is not easy to come by and even harder to identify. Typical RFPs use the words 'agencies.' While agencies may provide some of the services required for developing a destination brand strategy, it may be a conflict of interest for the company currently doing the advertising or promotional campaign to do the assessment and create the promise. Many advertising agencies or graphic design firms believe that they are in the business of brand development, and indeed some are. However, the real question to ask is: What is the vendor selling – advertising, graphic design or strategy? Ask yourself, if you were developing an RFP for a large bridge project, would you solicit construction firms to do the engineering? Of course not. You want the expertise of an independent expert to design the critical elements for success. True brand strategy requires the same high level of expertise." [12]

In some cases, unsuspecting locals have been lured by the glitz of the advertising examples and designs presented by agencies, causing them to lose sight of their original Request for Proposal (RFP) and the role of advertising and designs in the development of their tourism or branding strategy.

We understand why ambitious cities have great advertising, designs and communications. But these actions come after the overall strategic framework is established. The first step is to distill a competitive brand platform as the foundation on which everything will be built. Otherwise, it is like engaging a painter to design your home because you like the color he chooses and how he will finish the job without having established the right architecture with a specialist architect.

Managing the Selection Process

The selection process adopted by cities varies considerably. Some are able to make a direct appointment while others use a bid-type process, most often involving an RFP. An RFP invites competitive bids from firms for the delivery of specific outcomes in the most cost effective manner by the most qualified and appropriate provider. However, the RFP process, while a firmly entrenched procedure by government and other organizations, does not guarantee the best outcome. In fact, I believe that it too often works against the city's best interests. Some cities are in the fortunate position of being able to research and appoint their preferred brand strategy consultant without having to undertake a competitive bidding process.

Many RFPs are not well written, are generic, and usually contain no budget details or are loaded with the terms that have been borrowed from the sales materials of a firm, thereby hinting that the selection is a foregone conclusion. They are also frequently weighed down by rules and requirements, and not focused on a clear explanation of the situation, problem and objectives at hand.

RFPs demand a large time (and cost) commitment from all concerned. For consultants, the preparation of an RFP response usually takes days, even weeks, of executive time. Not to mention the possible time and expense needed to attend a presentation. Hence, the decision by consultants as to whether to respond to an RFP has to be taken very seriously.

Knowing the budget or budget range for the project is extremely important to the consultancy. Yet, too few RFPs contain this information. Would you walk into a car dealership and not tell the salesperson approximately how much you are looking to spend? How is the salesperson to know if you want a luxury or standard model? Yet, the equivalent of this happens every day when cities do not disclose their budget and leaves the consultancy to play a guessing game in trying to estimate the budget and scope of services that they should include in their response. A better approach is to disclose the budget and then evaluate the proposed deliverables according to their appropriateness, quality and value.

A preferable alternative to the RFP is a Request for Qualifications (RFQ) or Request for Information (RFI). This involves a two-step approach which initially evaluates the credentials and capabilities of firms, then commencing discussions and negotiations with the most qualified and appropriate respondent. If these discussions are not successful, the next most qualified firm can then be contacted.

Tips for Evaluating Vendors

The task of evaluating vendors and their proposals can be tricky. Your capacity and that of your committee will be strengthened if everyone is knowledgeable about what contributes toward successful place brands and how to evaluate various types of firms. The current economic climate makes this all the more acute because it is encouraging firms to broaden their market focus by offering new services to weather the storm. We have recently seen advertising, web design vendors and communications agencies pitch for the development of tourism and brand strategies for cities and regions. Unfortunately, few of these agencies had any tourism or place branding credentials. This can create confusion for city leaders or panelists on a selection committee.

A successful outcome for your brand planning will be greatly enhanced if there is a good fit between the consultancy, your team and the community. The following are just a few points to bear in mind when evaluating the credentials of RFP respondents.

Their Methodology

- Does the firm have past experience in creating a place branding strategy, i.e. beyond advertising, websites or logos?

- Do they have a clear and logical process to guide place branding?
- Ask their past place branding clients about their process. What went well? What didn't? Why?
- Does their research provide insights into the attitudes, perceptions and feelings of external audiences?
- Is there an over-emphasis on the buying characteristics of the local community?
- Are they overselling the value of their research? How much of it is repackaged from third party vendors and can be acquired by you for a few hundred dollars?

Their Track Record

- Which places have they worked for? What did they do?
- Does their positioning always present a valuable and competitive proposition for external audiences? Or is it often "warm and fuzzy" and possibly designed to make locals feel good about themselves? Or is their recommended positioning generic and could be used by almost any other place?
- When checking references be sure that you are comparing apples with apples. While it is a good idea to seek the opinion of colleagues, friends and other associates in general, it is advisable to obtain recommendations and references from the firm's past clients with similar composition and dynamics to your city.
- Take the time to thoroughly search online for media reports regarding prospective firms and their senior executives to see if they have had any relevant controversies. Has their work generated controversy for past clients more than once? What was the nature of the controversy? While a disgruntled resident or over-zealous reporter can generate unwarranted negative media coverage, it does pay to fully understand the controversy. Is there a pattern of negative comments?
- Ask past clients if the firm stayed within the agreed timeline and budget. Did they try to increase the budget after the work

commenced? How long did it take them to complete the strategy? Most firms take 6-9 months.

Their Real Team

- Don't assume that going to the biggest, well-known firm is best. You may find yourself assigned to the sandpit where their C team can learn the ropes. Who will actually do the work for you? It is not uncommon for large agencies to do a bait and switch, after selling you on the credentials of their A team, they allocate a more inexperienced team to actually do the work.
- What role will the principal of the organization and the team making the presentation play? Be wary of those that send in their sales team to make the pitch. They will probably hit the ball out of the park – but that's what they are employed to do! You may never see or speak to them again because others will be assigned to the project. Make sure that you meet or talk to the team allocated to do the work and lead the project on a daily basis. These are the people who will be responsible for your success.
- What is the depth of experience of their individual team members in tourism, economic development and place branding and marketing?
- Keep in mind that all large firms claim a client list that predates most of their current staff. What places have the proposed individuals actually worked on and exactly what did they do on those projects?
- How many other projects will the lead team members be working on at the same time as yours? If more than three or four, you may be signing on to a branding factory.

The Price

- Price shouldn't be the final consideration. Neither the most expensive nor the cheapest should be disregarded on the basis of price alone. We have seen organizations discard the lowest priced options because some of their committee felt "you have to pay a high price to get the best."

- A firm's capabilities, experience, and relevance to projects does vary. Don't think that all vendors are the same; therefore you can choose the one with the lowest price and save. Where this philosophy is adopted it ends up costing the city more in the end when they have to fix what was poorly done. Others have ended up with a brand that has little or no meaning and never fulfills the project objectives. And not to mention the lead organization's lost credibility and an opportunity that may be lost for another decade.

Beware of Bright Shiny Objects

- Avoid the mistake of selecting a firm on the basis of their attractive print advertising examples. The selection of the best of these agencies to create your advertising, communications or graphics should be made **after** you have established your brand strategy.
- Be particularly careful when you see full page ads featuring small cities used as examples in proposals. These have most likely never been used as part of a campaign because the communities do not have the funds to run them. Yet, it's amazing how many committees are lured by an agency's attractive advertising examples when the city only has a tiny advertising budget. Instead, you should be evaluating firms solely on the basis of their ability to define a competitive, distinctive and deliverable brand. Beware of bright shiny objects! They are often irrelevant to the job at hand.

CHAPTER SEVEN

The Seven Steps to a Place Brand

It is remarkable how many places rush to define their new brand following one or two brainstorming sessions that may have involved only the lead organization's staff, a few stakeholders and a graphic design agency. Equally as dangerous is when the agency presents only a new logo and tagline to the DMO and stakeholders and calls it a brand strategy. Sometimes the approach is to first design brand elements, then sell them to constituents. Efforts like these usually fail to ignite enthusiasm among stakeholders and partners and quickly run out of steam. When launched, the brand does not have the support of key stakeholders because they were not treated as valued partners from the start. Sometimes it is not only a matter of what you do, but how you go about doing it. Our experience has shown that the collaborative and consultative approach leads to a stronger and much more sustainable brand.

In Durham NC, Shelly Green, CEO at the Convention & Visitors Bureau, encouraged broad community buy-in when conducting the Durham's brand planning. She advises, "The key to avoiding controversy is to involve as many people and organizations in the process as possible and by doing this everyone has had a say, so they find it hard to criticize at the end. I think that we did this very successfully and the controversy and complaints for us were almost zero."

Formulating a new brand can take five to twelve months or more, depending upon the size of the community, research required, level of consultation, the decision-making process and the speed of decisions and approvals along the way.

The 7A Destination Branding Process

The 7A Destination Branding Process recognizes the special nature of community-based branding. While it was originally developed for tourism, it is applicable to all forms of place branding – including nations. It encourages a holistic approach that harnesses stakeholder buy-in from the start and examines the world in which the brand must excel. This is essential to generate understanding and enthusiasm for the new brand. Importantly, it reinforces the need to build the brand from the inside out and ensures that planners are exposed to the heart and soul of the community, as well as the strengths of competitors and dynamics of the marketplace. 7A has been formulated around four core principles – strategic research and analysis, brand strategy, competitive identity, and brand communication and delivery.

Figure 1: The 7A Destination Branding Process

The steps in the 7A Destination Branding Process and the critical questions that must be answered are:

1. **Assessment and Audit**	What is the city's place in the world?
2. **Analysis and Advantage**	What will the city be known for?
3. **Alignment**	What are the brand's relationships?
4. **Articulate**	How will the brand be expressed visually and verbally?
5. **Activation**	How will the brand come to life?
6. **Adoption and Attitudes**	How can stakeholders support the brand?
7. **Action and Afterward**	How will the brand be managed and kept fresh and relevant?

The rigor and speed with which you complete all seven steps will be influenced by the size of your community, its stage of development, scope of the brand, politics, available budget, time, and the authority and autonomy with which the lead organization and brand committee have been empowered to make decisions.

Communities that have followed this path find it transformational because it is energizing, educational, and a great unifying force. Most experience unexpected bonuses such as renewed support, revitalized relationships, and a rekindled sense of community purpose. It also serves to establish the lead organization as an important community leader and as a future-focused organization.

As you proceed through each step, you will find that it is likely to be an iterative route and that things may not necessarily proceed in a smooth, linear fashion. At times you may be engaged in more than one step at a time. You may also need to return to an earlier step due to findings and solutions that are revealed at a later stage. This also strengthens the brand because maintaining flexibility and openness contributes to a much stronger and healthier result.

CHAPTER EIGHT

Step One: Assessment – What's Your Place in the World?

This first step is extremely important and is often the longest phase because it involves thoroughly reviewing and analyzing the world in which the brand must excel. It establishes the knowledge base and foundation for everything that follows.

How you approach this step depends upon the size of the place, its dynamics, past marketing efforts, and the available budget. Your actions will also be influenced by the relevance, quantity and availability of existing reports, past research, strategies, and publications, as well as the new research that is commissioned. How readily the community has participated in activities like this in the past will also influence the approach that you take. These steps should uncover the current status of the city's marketing and image, where it came from, and the position that it needs to occupy in the future.

There are four basic questions that need to be answered:

- Who do we think we are?
- Who do our customers think we are?
- Who do we want to become?
- Who are we most likely to become?

During this step you will be taking 'snapshots' of the current scene. It pays to be objective while sifting through this valuable information. Avoid jumping to premature conclusions, taking shortcuts, or falling in love with early ideas as this may compromise your thinking. Maintaining an open mind will enable you to capture a more accurate picture of where the brand is today, and where it can possibly go in future.

Information overload may set in quickly as you filter the material from many sources including the disparate attitudes, values, opinions, needs, and arguments that you may hear – sometimes all within one meeting!

While it may be tempting, don't bypass or minimize the importance of Step One. Setting your foot in the wrong place at this stage may cause you to be miles off course when you start revealing the rest of the identity. Keep an open mind, look for unexpected gems, and don't let politics and parochialism overshadow the views and needs of external customers. At times there may be temptations and pressure to go faster or to skip some steps. Just as a great chef won't sacrifice quality for speed, you must have the same philosophy.

Revealing the brand relies on objective research and analysis, and a lot of creative thinking and collaboration. Michelangelo, one of the greatest sculptors of all time, described his skill as the ability to remove marble, chip by chip, to reveal the shape that was already residing within the stone. You could consider your brand as also "encased in stone" in the form of features, attitudes, thoughts, benefits, personality, perceptions, experiences, and many irrelevant pieces. To find the masterpiece inside, you must chip away at the information, issues, components and distractions until you expose the competitive identity and most potent brand essence within. You are not creating the brand essence. It already exists. Your task is to reveal it!

Research: How to Obtain Answers to Your Questions

It is surprising how many places are flying blind when it comes to knowing their customers and their marketing environment. One of the greatest hurdles is the lack of actionable research to support their decision-making. Therefore, decisions are often based totally on "conventional wisdom" that later proves to be unreliable. It is impossible to know what customers think and feel without some form of research. Simply put, the more committed that cities can be to their research efforts, the better prepared they are to make informed and objective decisions.

Research doesn't have to be a complex, expensive, or wasteful exercise. Consider it as a systematic way to gather needed facts and information. No matter the size of your budget, it comes down to asking the right questions of the right people, under the right conditions. Even when we apply this simple definition, many places still struggle because they don't have even a basic information gathering system in place.

John Kelsh, Principal with Seattle-based Great Destination Strategies stresses the important role of research, "Because a place brand is what others think of it, market research is essential in three important ways. First by understanding the visitor's baseline image of who you are now, secondly by understanding which of your assets are most compelling, and thirdly by gauging perceptions of your brand relative to competitors. Unfortunately, too many places try to avoid some of these actions. Today we can achieve all of them even with modest budgets."

We agree that it's a challenge for small cities to budget for sophisticated research projects, but it shouldn't mean that they abandon all efforts. They can employ a range of cost effective research techniques and while they may not be as comprehensive as some conducted for larger places, they are certainly better than flying blind. Examples of ways in which research can be used to inform your brand development decisions include:

- Assessing the status of the current brand
- Identifying priority markets, their demographics and behavioral characteristics
- Gauging perceptions and attitudes toward the place
- Assessing competitors
- Identifying and testing the city's ideal positioning
- Assessing customer satisfaction
- Selecting and testing taglines and logos
- Monitoring brand performance

A basic research program provides a wealth of valuable information that will result in a much stronger brand than simply going on gut instinct and a few opinions. The smaller your marketing budget, the smaller your margin for error and the more imperative it is for you to make absolutely certain that you are allocating valuable resources on the right markets and customers, and employing the right messages.

Brad Dean, CEO of Myrtle Beach Area Chamber of Commerce confirms the importance of this, "Our customized approach to research has been extremely helpful for us to stay on top of what consumers are responding to in regard to our brand. Thanks to this ongoing strategic research, we've been able to adapt messaging when needed and stay current on what our consumers are most likely to respond to. It also helps in fine-tuning our marketing decisions based on current trends when it comes to media selection, messaging, and has allowed us to stay comprehensive in the way we reach our consumers and target markets."

Research should reveal what your customers like and dislike. It can be tempting to nudge the customer's views aside in favor of the opinions of locals, but the brand will ultimately gain greater traction and sustainability when there has been a concerted effort to understand the customer's needs, desires, likes and dislikes. Your options can be broadly divided into two forms of research collection: primary and secondary.

Primary Research

Primary research is the data and findings that you originate yourself. It may be conducted by you or by engaging a specialist. Some of the common methods include:

Consumer Perceptions Research

These studies enable comparison and evaluation of the city in regard to competitors by using criteria and attributes that are important to the customer. While comprehensive perception studies may be outside of the available budget of some small cities, there are a number of cost-effective options available.

Face-to-Face Interviews

Interviews with residents, business owners and community

leaders as well as external partners such as meeting planners can provide invaluable insights. The information gathered in these interviews is often not possible to obtain from focus groups and workshops. It is sometimes better to engage some constituents through these interviews because they may be reluctant to express their true thoughts and feelings in a public forum. This particularly applies to political and business leaders, or critics of the DMO or city government.

Focus Groups and Workshops

These meetings can be conducted in the city or in source markets with prospective customers, and usually comprise eight to fifteen participants. Topics for discussion include attitudes toward the city, potential positioning and brand platform options, and can provide input in regard to gaps in brand experiences. Focus groups can also be valuable for exploring reactions toward ideas and solutions.

Community Forums

One of the benefits of this forum is to provide a large number of interested people the opportunity to directly participate in the process. Depending upon the community, the number of participants may range from thirty to more than a hundred. The downside of these forums is that the large number of participants can be a deterrent for those wishing to express their true feelings, or it may be dominated by a few outspoken individuals. A skilled facilitator can mitigate these issues.

Stakeholder Survey

Those who cannot join interviews, workshops, or forums, may be able to participate in a survey or poll. Affordable online options such as Surveymonkey.com and Zoomerang.com provide powerful Internet-based survey and analytical tools that are ideal for small communities.

Secondary Research

Sometimes called desk research, secondary research generally involves the review and analysis of published information, data and reports that are readily available. This is less costly than primary research, but will not provide the customized information available through primary research.

Valuable secondary information can be obtained by reviewing information relevant to:

- Trends and transactions relating to lodging, tourism, relocation, and economic development.
- Tourism, cultural, economic development, and other relevant research that has been completed in recent years.
- Past marketing, collateral materials, websites and third party promotion, e.g. National, state and regional offices, commercial guidebooks, tour operator brochures, and material from the local tourism industry.
- Local and relevant media archives to assess their coverage of the city, customer groups, and competitors.
- Social media and user-generated sites.

Take A 360° View

During the Assessment step, the idea is to take an unbiased 360 degree view to gain an understanding of internal and external customers, their needs, competitor capabilities, and uncover distinctive strengths, trends, customer experiences, attitudes, personality and the capabilities of the city.

An honest self-examination is essential and requires an objective appraisal of not only the strengths, but also areas where the city may be considered deficient or weak. This may be difficult for some locals to admit. However, without this honesty, the brand could be considerably weakened and short-lived. Among the perspectives that should be evaluated are:

1. Target Audiences
2. Internal Stakeholders
3. Strengths and Assets

- *The Intangibles*: These include the city's ambience, community pride, personality, authenticity, image, reputation, sensory stimulation and celebrity.

4. Sense of Place: Is It Different and Comfortable?

The city's distinctive sense of place and how it functions is critical to its appeal and sustainability. The appearance of the city sends strong messages to visitors and newcomers as they walk or drive through its streets. The National Trust for Historic Preservation refers to a sense of place as "those things that add up to a feeling that a community is a special place, distinct from anywhere else." [13] While it may not represent a vital element in the brand platform, the community's sense of place itself is relevant because, at the least, it forms an important backdrop for where people will experience the brand. In many cases this involves the city center which often reflects the heart and soul of the community and plays an important role in what people may think of the place in general. In order to assess these qualities, experience the place from a customer's perspective. Take time to walk the streets, drive around, visit sporting facilities, check out attractions, use public facilities, spend time in public spaces and review future development plans. What is the visual and physical connectivity like within the area? Is it conducive to relaxing and spending time? Is it a gathering place and favorable to meeting and socializing? Is there a positive sense of welcome?

5. Performance: What Has Been Achieved?

Reviewing a wide variety of metrics will provide insights into the strengths, weaknesses and opportunities facing the city. Some of the questions that you should consider include:

- How has the city performed in recent years?
- Have competitors performed the same, worse or better?
- Have new industries or businesses emerged or declined?
- Are surveys available that monitor customer opinions, attitudes and satisfaction?

After examining available data, you should be able to uncover issues relating to seasonality, source markets, market share, length of stay, yield, and visitor dispersal throughout the area.

6. Communications Audit: What Does It Reveal?

A communications audit provides an understanding of the creativity, content, consistency, and effectiveness of current and past communications produced by the city's leading place marketers.

Start by assembling past advertising, websites, trade show displays, brochures, photo images, and media clippings to review content, themes, design, and style. Don't forget about the marketing communications of key partners. Next, review the results of past marketing efforts, including analysis of web traffic, advertising responses, and conversion rates and inquiries from prospective customers as well as customer complaints. What worked? What didn't? Examine the content of articles and features on the city to identify themes, accuracy, and tone of the coverage.

7. External Stakeholders: What Are They Thinking?

There are frequently important individuals and organizations outside the city who play a pivotal role in influencing perceptions of the area. They often have a very deep understanding of the place with an objectivity and customer focus that local residents don't always have. They can more readily identify the blemishes, as well as the opportunities and strengths that can lead to improved performance.

Members of the city's distribution channels should be involved in the research. It may seem somewhat strange to use the term 'distribution' because tourism and economic development products can't be stored and transported like food or consumer goods. However, distribution is the term used to describe the vital information, sales, and transaction links between a place and its end-customers. This network of intermediaries enables it to reach and influence distant target audiences. They may involve packaging and promoting tourism products to the area, selling real estate, planning conferences, and events or providing advice on relocation.

8. Competitors: How Do We Stack Up?

Knowing exactly who your competitors are can be more involved than it might first appear. Many cities simply regard their competitors as the places that are in their immediate vicinity or every other place in the universe. This overlooks the underlying factors that may be motivating customers and the myriad options they have. The reality is that it's your customers who determine who your competitors are. Your competitors are very likely to change depending upon the specific market segments you're addressing and may even change depending on the time of year. For example, Whistler B.C. (Canada) attracts snow sport enthusiasts during winter, as well as a wide variety of outdoor enthusiasts and sightseers during the other months. This brings them into competition with different places at different times of the year.

Sources of competitor intelligence include:

- Analysis of advertising, websites and other material.
- First-hand experience as a visitor, and observations and experiences of your staff and partners.
- Travel products such as packages, cruises, and tours.
- The marketing activities and offerings of the organizations in the competitor city.
- Media coverage including trade publications.
- Statewide economic and tourism performance trends.
- Statistical data.
- User generated sites and other social media

9. Experiences: How Are We Doing at Critical Moments?

Quite simply a brand is a promise. To be even more precise, it is the promise of a valued experience that must be kept, because the essential core of the brand is how it will make customers think and feel. This is why place branding requires a 360° focus to address the customer's total experience.

A corporate brand may have anywhere from five to fifty points where it is in touch with its customers. On the other hand, the number for a place brand could be endless because there is no limit to the points where customers interact with it. Beyond the obvious hotels, restaurants, shops, information centers and airport, a city can touch customers through the weather, the media, its citizens, as well as through friends and relatives, and even health providers and supermarkets. Many of the contact points are out of the direct control of the lead organization and its individual branding partners.

If you've been attracted to a place by its advertising, and then experienced vague reservations agents, untidy streets, poor service, and uninteresting atractions, then you know that there are more important priorities for places like this than an advertising campaign to attract more visitors. These places are leaking income, jobs, taxes and reputation – not to mention brand equity. Nothing can "kill" a place with inferior experiences faster than effective promotion. The more people are lured to a place like this and are exposed to its inadequacies, the faster and wider the negative word of mouth will spread, precipitating a rapid downward spiral.

Unlike a corporate manager, the city's brand manager must work with many more organizations and individuals over whom he or she usually has no control or authority, let alone the ability to request conformity to the city's brand platform and guidelines. They must, however, try to influence quality at the most critical moments of contact with visitors and customers.

Later in the process it will be necessary to revisit this audit to identify the actions needed at critical points of contact. Is there a focus on how people feel? Are there gaps? What are the causes of the gaps? What are the underlying problems?

10. Trends: Which Wave Will You Catch?

If you have ever been surfing, then you know that timing is everything. Catching a wave at the right moment can be the experience of a lifetime. On the other hand, bad timing can result in being dumped and surfacing with a mouth full of sand. Branding can be a lot like that! If you catch a trend moving in the wrong direction, it can be much the same as being dumped by a wave. Aligning with a strong trend, however can add charisma, celebrity and prosperity to your brand. Cultural and economic trends can have a profound influence on customer tastes and preferences. Are there economic, social, cultural and technical trends likely to help or hinder the acceptance and performance of your brand?

Questions

- What is distinctive and compelling, and competitors can't easily match?
- What is it like to be a customer of your community?
- What are the perceptions and attitudes toward your city?
- What is the vision for the community?
- What are the content, tone, and trend of media articles and coverage of the city?
- What were the results of past marketing efforts?
- How are the city's external markets structured?
- Who are the main and secondary competitors?
- How does the competitor set change for each market?

CHAPTER NINE

Step Two: Analysis and Advantage – What Will You Be Known For?

Thoroughly analyzing all of the information and data collated in Step One will provide a realistic picture of the brand's dimensions and what is needed to address any gaps and shortcomings. Most importantly, it sets the stage to claim your positioning and competitive advantage, and for defining the objectives and strategies needed to build the brand.

Stake Your Claim

Positioning a place or destination requires careful consideration of three dynamic elements, for which you have already collated the relevant information. These are (1) the needs of target customers, (2) place strengths (both tangible and intangible), and (3) competitor strengths. The recommended positioning should only be finalized after community values and vision have been taken into account. A SWOT Analysis (Strengths, Weaknesses, Opportunities and Threats) is one of the tools that can assist in the analysis.

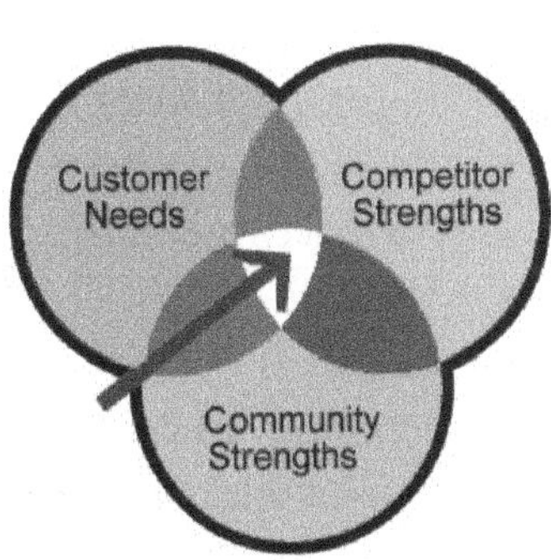

Figure 2: Opportunity Modeling for Optimum Positioning

Figure 2 illustrates the process of opportunity modeling in which filtering and refining the wealth of qualitative and quantitative information leads to defining the optimal positioning. The strongest positioning is at the intersection of these three concentric circles. This is where you aim to establish the most meaningful edge or competitive advantage that others can't easily match. You must be hard-nosed about identifying the distinctive strengths that match market needs and wants. At this point you must be extra vigilant to ensure that weak elements don't start slipping into the proposition simply to keep everyone happy. You will also need to identify and address how the weaknesses can be neutralized or turned into strengths.

Your most powerful positioning should place the city outside of the gravitational field of competitors, yet where it can resonate with greatest clarity and relevance for key audiences. If it is not clearly differentiated or remains in the shadow of major competitors, the city will always be seen as a pale alternative, and proving its differences, relevance and added value will become increasingly difficult. Competing head to head with more formidable competitors with similar positioning and value proposition is never sustainable.

The following are some of the variables commonly used to position a place. At times it requires a combination of them to claim the most distinctive and potent point of difference.

- Architecture and design
- Attractions
- Celebrity and fame
- Climate
- Cuisine and wine
- Culture
- Emotional benefits and feelings
- Ethnicity
- Events
- History
- Industry and local products
- Influence and power
- Landmarks and icons
- Legends and myths
- Location and access
- Natural environment
- Nightlife
- People
- Personality and values
- Physical attributes
- Social benefits
- Sport

The Criteria for Power Positioning

During the opportunity modeling phase, each positioning option should be evaluated against the following four criteria.

Differentiation: Strong brands stand out from the crowd and are different in ways that are valued and relevant to customers. How important is your point of difference? Is it valuable enough to allow you to charge a premium price? Will it allow you to lead with products and experiences that competitors can't easily match? Will you be seen as the only or best choice based on this proposition?

Compelling: In order to be relevant, the positioning must be more than just different. If the difference is not sufficiently compelling to stimulate or peak customer's interest it will not stimulate demand. Being the *Grass Seed Capital of the World* may mark Linn County OR as different, but is it attractive to external customers? The positioning needs to be based on attributes that will be most effective at hitting customer hot buttons that are valued and are meaningful.

Truthful: A sustainable brand must be true to itself and not attempt to present itself as something it's not. Is the positioning credible, authentic and believable? Can you always deliver on this promise? For instance, is the place trying to position itself as a cultural city, but without an active or prosperous arts community or quality events?

Sustainable: Is this a short term proposition based on a current trend or fad? Or is this closely associated with the core essence of the place and how locals see themselves? Will it unify stakeholders? Will it last in tough times? Can it survive more than one electoral or budget cycle? Is it sustainable from an environmental perspective? Is it dependent upon some businesses or organizations that are rather insecure? Is the brand dependent upon future major investments? How will the brand be impacted if the investments do not occur in a timely manner? Does it create opportunities for new products and businesses?

Brand Positioning: Claiming the Most Valuable Real Estate

A city's most valuable real estate is not the largest buildings that form its skyline. Rather, it is the space in the hearts and minds of its customers where they store all of their thoughts, feelings, and perceptions about the place. This is the territory that influences where they will visit, work, live, shop, invest or study, and where you find the memories and feelings that build respect and give preference over competitors. Your challenge is to stake your claim on the most valuable piece of this real estate. This is *positioning*, and represents how you want customers to think and feel about the place. It is how the city's key stakeholders want targeted customers to see it relative to other options.

In the hundreds of destination marketing plans that we have reviewed over the years, we are surprised to find that so few of them include positioning. One of the great advantages of a structured planning approach, such as our *7A Process*, is that it forces consideration of this pivotal building block.

Defining your city's brand position is, without a doubt, the most important and trickiest part of the entire place branding process. The task of pinpointing the most competitive positioning should receive thorough consideration. If you don't get this part right, everything else will miss its mark, since it is the positioning and its relevance to target audiences that informs and shapes all other elements of the brand.

Another way to consider the role of positioning and branding is to think of it as what you want the city to be known for, and the role of the branding and marketing programs as being the means to secure and reinforce it in the hearts and minds of customers. The best positioning is based <u>on a single thought or idea</u>. This is genuinely difficult for most places to agree upon because of the complex matrix of products, markets and stakeholders that it's trying to satisfy. Not to mention an overabundance of competitors. It involves examining the context and space in which the city fits into the customer's world. If you are serious, there is no shortcut or room for politics, parochialism, appeasement or self-interest. This is quite a challenge when there are many competing voices, but it is essential that you avoid watered down and meaningless positioning. The strongest positioning often means a degree of sacrifice and sometimes unpopular decisions. The city must single-mindedly zero in on its one core truth, DNA or essence that will connect customers with the city's most compelling and competitive experiences. This may involve a combination or blend of a few attributes, characteristics or benefits to provide the originality or distinctiveness that will strike a chord.

Unique: To Be, or Not To Be?
Being unique simply means "the only one of its kind." Does that mean unique in the entire world? The overused term "unique" is so misused and worn-out, and above all, a status that is very difficult to achieve. Among the 20,000 incorporated cities in the USA, there are few that can claim to be truly unique on the basis of characteristics that are important to customers. Identifying the ideal positioning must be considered in the context of the audience that the community is trying to influence and within the set of competitors that the customer may consider. Regardless, some will insist that all cities are unique, like fingerprints or snowflakes, no two are exactly the same. While some consumer products or fast moving goods can claim a positioning that is truly unique, this is much harder for cities because they have many more competitors. Not only are so many of them physically alike, many of them even have the same names. For example, there are 150 Jacksons, 101 Lincolns, and 57 Springfields in the United States.

While major cities such as London, New York, Sydney, Hong Kong, and Rio de Janeiro battle within the global context, most small cities should be more narrowly focused on expressing their edge within their competitor set. This usually involves comparisons to places closer to home. Does it matter if a small city in Utah is positioning itself as the place for enjoying the therapies and relaxation of herbal gardens when there are places in Vermont and Florida doing the same? It probably doesn't because their target markets are within their immediate regions. However, these cities should never have the same or similar tagline!

Parity Isn't a Winning Position
Wherever they go, visitors expect to find high quality lodging, good restaurants, well-designed public spaces,

and friendly people. Avoid positioning that is based on entry-level attributes or points of parity that are simply expected of all places. If an attribute is a threshold requirement, i.e. friendliness, good service, attractive prices or cleanliness, it is unlikely to represent a meaningful differentiating factor that will deliver added value or sustainable positioning.

Ed Burghard at Strengthening Brand America observes, "It has been my observation economic development professionals tend to get tripped up by attempting to position their community as the best location choice because they have everything a company needs to be successful. The fact is all companies require certain category benefits like a great business climate, affordable and skilled labor, reliable telecom systems, etc. These are simply 'tickets to entry.' All locations under consideration will offer these category benefits. Dr. Kevin Lane Keller (Dartmouth College) would characterize these as points of parity. What communities need to figure out is what their relevant and competitive points of difference are. Typically, a community will find their most compelling points of difference reflect the unique asset collection, infrastructure and/or public policies that enable delivery of the desired category benefit. In short, communities compete less on WHAT they deliver and more on uniquely HOW they deliver the category benefit. They have a legitimate chance at owning the HOW, but likely not the WHAT."

Neil Lee at The Work Foundation in the UK says, "Like all strategies, distinctiveness needs careful handling. It is easy for distinctiveness to fall victim to gimmicks or to unrealistic thinking. Yet when it is used as a catalyst for regeneration, and used to fit into wider economic strategies, distinctiveness has the capacity to transform the success of a city. The example of Bilbao (Spain) is one indication of what is possible. Bilbao built the Guggenheim, but it was successful because it was accompanied by the redevelopment of the airport and the building of a new metro system. Place branding always works best when it points to an underlying, concrete reality of difference." [14]

While a place may have defined its individual characteristics and decided to position them as distinctive, a more objective and honest assessment might reveal that they are also common to many nearby places. For example, in the Pacific Northwest many communities pin their positioning on their natural scenery, mountains, or a high quality of life. The reality is that nearly all communities in the Pacific Northwest are natural, beautiful, and enjoy a high quality of life. These qualities are almost the price of admission to play the game in this region. Those that want to base their positioning on their natural environment or quality of life had better have superiority in some other aspect of these experiences. "Pretty much everyone's got rivers and mountains in Washington," the mayor of Snoqualmie WA said. "The question is 'How do you set yourself apart?" [15]

Similarly, cities in California and Florida have to provide much more than sunny weather, and cities in Arizona need more than easy access to high quality golf courses and desert scenery. The congestion in positioning options can also be seen in rugged outdoor locations. For example, Anchorage AK and near neighbor The Yukon, Canada both covet the "larger than life" positioning that is important to their adventure-seeking visitors. This crowded position is highlighted by the similarity of Anchorage's tagline *Big. Wild. Life* and The Yukon's *Larger than Life*.

No, You Can't Have – or Be – It All!

The decision as to which components should lead the positioning can be controversial. Obviously, not all aspects are of equal interest and value to customers. For this reason, the city must lead with those that will best attract, motivate, and satisfy target audiences. Too often, the ideal point of difference becomes blurred and diluted by a lack of consensus, or when the "We have everything," "It's all here," or "The center (or heart) of it all" syndrome emerges.

The "we have everything" syndrome is one of the most common pitfalls in securing strong positioning. The idea may play well to locals and be seen as a good compromise because it is inclusive and seems to make everyone in the community happy (a dead giveaway you're on the wrong track!). But compromising just to make locals feel good, without resonating positively with external customers is the absolute antithesis of what good positioning and branding is about.

Not even the largest places can be all things to all people. New York City realizes that it doesn't have resorts, ski slopes, natural wonders and wineries. Successful place brands are those that are able to clearly differentiate themselves, hit customer hot buttons, and are a unifying force for stakeholders. Fundamental to achieving this is for participants to take an objective, customer-focused view and play their very strongest hand – even if some can't be the star of the show.

Whisper Brand Strategy Consultants presents a very strong critique of these warm and fuzzy taglines, saying, "Adulatory claims and *cheerleader messages* gain credibility among those on the inside responsible for the brand – executives, members and other organizational leaders. They feel great about these cheerleader messages because they are so darn POSITIVE. But each of these insiders is already convinced – they are paid to pay attention – while the outside consumer they wish to influence is not. Consumers are unlikely to invest time or public money when a brand shouts in self-flattery ....which is why they are so numbingly unmemorable, and irrelevant." [16]

Sadly, it's not difficult to find dozens of high priced brand strategies with positioning that is so self-congratulatory that I can only surmise they were chosen to keep the locals happy. These are a waste of time and public money. Someone was not asking the simple customer-focused questions, such as "What's in it for me?"

And It's Not Enough to Be "A Great Place to Live, Work and Play"!

We rarely conduct a brand workshop for a community when someone doesn't say, "this is the best place to live, work and play." Further, many advocate that it should be the city's tagline. Cities that do not use objective outsiders to assist their planning often pat themselves on the back and agree that they've found the Holy Grail – and "a great place to live, work and play" it is.

I Googled the term and found over five million results. There are also about two hundred videos on YouTube with various community spokespersons using the term. I lost count of those using the term as a tagline. So if you are considering joining the masses in building a brand based on being "a great place to live, work and play," you have simply identified an essential requirement to play the game. There are tens of thousands of places that can match your claim. You have to dig deeper to uncover the true essence of the place that will be valued and meaningful to target audiences – and credible!

There's Money in Hot Dogs and Beer

As I said earlier, some community leaders and marketers find it difficult to agree on a single idea or concept on which to set their city apart. Their main fear is that something or someone will be left out. I like to use a baseball analogy to illustrate this dilemma. In baseball it seems that the best batters and pitchers receive just about all of the pre-game publicity. Many of these guys make millions of dollars a year. There is another group that gets no pregame publicity, but also make millions a year – the operators of the concession stands. The hot dogs and beer can be very enjoyable, but they are not going to motivate you to go to a game. However, it's just not baseball without them. They are integral to this all-American experience, yet you hear nothing of them until you go to the game. Both need each other. If the beer and hot dog sellers were the ones featured in the media and not the pitchers and batters, none of them would make as much income.

The lesson is that you lead with what is most relevant and enticing at the particular time when customers are making their decisions. Similarly, a city must initially be very narrowly focused on its most compelling message to attract attention, and then follow with supporting attractions, services and experiences. Putting them in the wrong order would be no different to hoping to fill baseball stadiums by featuring the hot dog and beer sellers on the sports pages.

Kari Westlund at Travel Lane County OR clearly had this philosophy in mind when she said, "As destination marketers we are blessed in having so many robust tools that at some point we do get the chance to tell just about everyone's story. We may not always perk them up to the lead story, but we can work with most of them without losing focus on our brand essence."

Intangibles Are Cool

No community is one-dimensional. It's always more than its physical attributes and features. It might also have a cool, relaxed, laid-back demeanor and celebrity that can be as attractive as its physical assets like the beach, jazz bars, outdoor restaurants, and galleries. It is often intangibles like culture, heritage, fun, adventure and atmosphere that have the most profound influence defining what makes the city distinctive and special.

Suburban sprawl, cookie cutter developments, and big box retail outlets are globally creating an urban sameness which can make it difficult for leaders to express the attractiveness, individuality and distinctiveness of their communities. "Why the sudden interest in distinctiveness by cities? For a long time, cities yearned for Wal-Marts and McDonalds," one planning expert told the Seattle Times. "Now that we have them and see what they mean to our community landscapes, we're realizing we need something different. We want our authenticity to show itself." [17] Increasingly, places need to explore their cultural and intangible dimensions in order to distinguish themselves.

So much of what cities offer is experiential, explaining why their product is mainly intangible. We don't actually purchase the street, harbor, or café. We experience them rather than possess them. What is important and memorable is how we connect to the city and how it makes us feel. The quaint city of Padukah OK is not positioned based on its pleasant old town feel, but how its residents are *distinctively creative*. Similarly, the brand positioning for England's North East is founded on the innovation and passion of its people. *Passionate People, Passionate Places* is the tagline representing the brand directed by One North East in a region-wide campaign covering all elements of the North East's business, education, culture and sports offerings.

Relying on physical attributes alone allows competitors to more easily copy, weaken or match your claims of superiority. There won't be another Grand Canyon, but features such as outdoor recreation, history and natural assets may be shared with other communities. Instead, strive to "own" a lucrative, higher-level intangible benefit or feeling that can be used in concert with the physical assets.

The Alamo, Riverwalk and other attractions of San Antonio TX are encapsulated in the four pillars of its brand, People. Pride. Passion. Promise. They are captured in the tagline, *Deep. In the Heart*, which is a line from the iconic song *Deep in the Heart of Texas* written in 1941 and subsequently recorded by many artists. The positioning is founded on the symbolic role that the city has played in American history, patriotism, heroism, and legend.

Shaoxing, China is an ancient water city with a rich 6,000 year history. Its brand positioning is based on it being a one-of-a-kind place because of its associations with the nation's ancient and historical times, and its contributions toward various forms of artistic expression, including calligraphy, fictional novels, and Yue opera. The positioning is encapsulated in the statement *Vintage China*.

Intangibles, particularly those linked to strong emotional or social benefits, enable places to form special bonds and promise enticing rewards. They also help form a more inclusive and flexible brand that embraces more local partners as opposed to a positioning that is based solely on physical attributes. For example, if Arlington TX had based its brand on its theme parks alone, it would have limited the number of local partners that could relate directly to the brand. But, by basing the brand on the emotional benefits of family fun and excitement, the city is able to offer a stronger and more meaningful set of experiences which include Texas Rangers baseball, museums, and recreation. Their tagline *"and the crowd goes wild!"* nicely sums up the fun and excitement that the city promises.

Leave Room to Grow

Because a city is constantly evolving, its positioning should be aspirational – that is, it's forward facing and needs room to grow. This allows for trends and developments that may have a profound effect on the brand. It should form the foundation for product development, placemaking and small business development.

Queenstown (New Zealand) has earned the title, *"The World Adventure Capital"* through the confluence of a stunning natural setting and constant innovation. The variety of terrain and the New Zealand spirit for adventure has fueled their innovation in tourism. For the past twenty years, the local destination marketing organization and the tourism industry have had a strong focus on developing new commercial adventure products to support their brand proposition and in the process invented some spectacular thrills. Among the commercial activities are jet boating (invented here in 1970), Zorbing (the hamster ball), cave tubing (black water rafting), monorail biking, river boarding, zip-lining, canyon swing, tandem sky-diving, snow-kiting, white-water sledging, and bungee jumping which started here in 1988. There are more than a dozen other commercial adventure activities in the area and more on the drawing board.

Bahia Blanca is the only port in Argentina accommodating heavy ships. It is the hub for the southern part of the country and has the country's largest petrochemical industry. This provides excellent growth opportunities, particularly in education and technology. The brand has been defined as *USB* i.e. *Una Sola Bahia* (Only One Bay) positioning the port as the universal connection, a play on the computer term, USB.

The Brand's Engine Room: The Brand Platform

The brand platform provides the foundation on which the Destination Promise™ and all future brand actions and experiences will be based. It is the nucleus or engine of the brand. Here we outline what the place believes it is, what it gives customers, and what makes it distinctive and gives it personality. These elements have been crystallized from the interviews, workshops, research and the analysis and filtering conducted during the opportunity modeling phase.

Target Audience: The first task is to define the target audience, as this step enables you to fine-tune the brand platform according to how it resonates with them. This can be tricky because of the inclination to target everybody. The best approach is throughly segmenting the market to ensure that you understand their specific needs, emotional drivers and hot buttons. What is the experience that various groups want to have? This process of splitting prospective customers into individual groups is termed market segmentation. It serves to group people who share a common level of interest with the same needs and desires. The principles of segmentation play a critical role in guiding your planning, implementation and competitive advantage because all future decisions will be filtered according to their relevance to your target audiences.

The components of the brand platform are:

Brand Vision: What is the vision held by city leaders for the future of the place in five or twenty years? How does this compare to the vision held by stakeholders? Is there a gap? Does it aspire to create a distinct competitive advantage or is it safe and bland? The vision created through the brand planning process can sometimes prove to be more practical and effective than many aspects of the city government's vision because that document is often full of "motherhood" statements to keep everyone happy and difficult to action.

The brand vision clarifies the high-level role that the brand (and maybe tourism) will play in the city achieving its long-term goals. The vision should guide the city administration's involvement in everything from land use planning to urban design and regulations for restaurants and retailers. It also provides partners with the directions on which to base future investment, growth and planning. The brand vision should not be the sole province of the mayor or CEO, although they may be among the first to have strong ideas and perspectives as to what it should be. While considering this aspect, it's important to identify where the brand's energy and passion are likely to come from. Are there individuals, experiences, and assets that are more ready to participate than others?

Tangible Benefits: A brand cannot be created for a place that is devoid of strengths, attractions and assets – it must have credible physical and functional assets and features that are valued by customers. These are the tangible strengths that describe what the city has or does best. These may include interesting exhibits at museums, ski slopes, wineries or affordable industrial land. Benefits such as these are often the easiest for competitors to claim, match or copy.

Core Experiences: These are the key experience categories in which the place excels. In economic development circles they are called 'clusters.' These experiences represent its value proposition and competitive edge for target audiences. They also form the building blocks for development, investment and the ways to enjoy the community's authentic character. Examples of core experience themes for tourism might include adventure, gardens, natural wonders, maritime heritage, cultural traditions, culinary or wellness. For economic development they might be technology, maritime services, oil production or aircraft manufacturing.

Emotional Benefits: Emotional benefits are the positive feelings that people receive from a place. While the tangible benefits may be enticing and important, they cannot create a deep relationship. Emotional benefits have the ability to connect with people and influence the way they feel and bond with their deepest needs and desires. They should fulfill the state of mind that visitors are seeking, such as enrichment, romance, escape or adventure.

Social Benefits: These are the benefits that reflect how people would like others to see them. They might also be called bragging rights and relate to the celebrity, cache, and prestige of the place. They connect to one's self esteem and the positive recognition from being associated with the place.

Personality: The brand personality is sometimes referred to as "look and feel" or "tone and style." The role of personality is highly strategic, powerful and influential. It describes the brand in human terms. Places such as Calgary (Canada), Cambridge (England), or Silicon Valley CA each have their own individual character and personality. No matter which city you consider, it won't take long before you are describing it in the same terms that you would use to describe a person. Personality is extremely important in branding because it influences the words, colors, style and tone of voice we use in expressing it in marketing applications. The personality traits may include being glamorous, industrious, creative or fun.

Brand Values: These are the principles that the city and its constituents believe in and live by. They are the values by which residents want their community to grow and be shared with others. It is possible that the community has never verbalized these thoughts until this process, even though they have probably been in play for a long time. They are frequently the reasons why a community is the way that it is. These could be the values that you hear repeated during local interviews and workshops because they reflect what the city does and does not want to become. Examples of brand values that constituents may value are environmental stewardship, safety, volunteerism, teamwork and forward thinking.

Brand Credentials: Have you noticed that people like to patronize restaurants that have been favorably reviewed by a critic or order a wine that has won many awards? And have you seen the boost that an Oscar can give to a movie? Well, the same principle applies to cities.

Credentials, whether they evolve from association with an event, famous person, or favorable review, can give people satisfying peace of mind and level of trust that make it easier to choose one place over another. Providing credentials that give customers the reasons to believe a city's positioning serves to strengthen its Destination Promise™. Brand credentials are particularly useful in place marketing where the prospective visitor is purchasing an intangible that cannot be tested or examined before their arrival. Brand credentials might include achievements, media acknowledgements, historical facts, endorsements from famous people and experts, or sites of important events.

Peggy Bendel, President of Bendel Communications International, is a firm believer in the value that credible, third-party endorsements can add to a place brand. "For those places cited on a

'Best Places to Live' or *'Best Beach Towns"* list, that means much more than if they said it themselves. If a media outlet says that a city is a great place to do business, that's more credible than its own advertising. These endorsements can play a valuable role for customers by validating the city's brand proposition."

The power of third-party sources is further reinforced by the results of research conducted by Development Counsellors International entitled, *Winning Strategies in Economic Development.* The study revealed the sources of information that most influenced the perceptions of corporate executives in regard to the business climate in other cities are dialogue with industry peers (50%), articles in newspapers and magazines (46%), and rankings/surveys (35%). [18]

Brand credentials, or reasons to believe, help test and bulletproof the Destination Promise™ and will ensure that your brand proposition is realistic and can offer a defendable point of difference. Brand credentials are at the heart of what other people really think about the place.

Brand Essence: The brand essence is the DNA code from which the brand's narrative can evolve. This is the basic building block or glue that informs and holds together all brand experiences and messages. In the case of Oshkosh WI, its consistency in hosting major events inspires its brand essence: Wisconsin's event city. This in turn is influencing its streetscapes, visitor experiences and economic development programs. Your brand essence may be summed up by saying, "our brand is about ......" For Holon (Israel) it is "the children's city," for Asheville NC it is "enriching your life" and Medford and the Rogue Valley (OR) is "great performances." These are not taglines, although they could be. They are concise encapsulations of what the brands are about.

Brand Associations: Brand associations are the attributes (positive, negative, and neutral) that come to mind when people are exposed to the brand name, tagline, symbols, or elements of a place. They amount to what your audiences know about the community and how they feel about investing time and money in it. Associations influence how we file and recall what we know about it. A city should aspire to have its positive attributes come to mind and be translated into highly valued benefits by its customers. For instance, the mention of New York City may instantly bring to mind dozens of the city's places, events, people, and activities, as well as being crowded, noisy, exciting, and a host of other descriptions. For most people, New York City has a richly painted canvas in their minds, even if they have never visited there.

On the other hand, associations can work in reverse. Consumers may think of a word, need, product, benefit or feeling which immediately triggers them to think of a city name. Achieving this level of positive name associations is the ultimate goal. To use the New York City example again, the thought of "outstanding theater" or "big city excitement" may bring New York City immediately to mind. The trick, of course, is to ensure that the destination is associated with positive benefits and preferably those that are integral to its brand identity. You don't want to be the place that comes to mind when pollution, crime, rip-offs, bad traffic, or the phrase "tourist trap" are mentioned.

It Takes an Emotional Edge

Consider some of the world's most powerful consumer brands like Nike, Harley-Davidson, Victoria's Secret, and Disney. If these brands were based only on their physical elements, they would be much the same as their competitors. Instead, they have differentiated themselves by connecting with the emotional needs of customers, creating strong bonds, expectations, trust and intangible rewards. The reward for Nike's customers may be a sense of achievement, and Victoria's Secret promises self-expression and confidence. People connect emotionally with brands when they stand for something that is important to them.

I agree with what fellow Australian Geoff Ayling said in *Rapid Response Advertising*, "There is only one reason why people have ever bought from you in the past, and why they will ever buy from you in the future, and that is because they want to change the way they feel. It's that simple."[19] The next time you walk around a resort, historic town, winery, or along a forest trail, look at the people around you. You will recognize that everyone you see is there to create or maintain a positive emotional state by feeling better in some way.

While Disney theme park guests connect through family freedom, Las Vegas is about adult freedom, and Reno NV has elements of both along with a sense of adventure in the outdoors surrounding the city. Unlike many consumer goods, cities can form rich and meaningful connections with their visitors. We become totally immersed and surrounded by them, sometimes for several days, and this can profoundly influence and stimulate our senses – and emotions.

When choosing a place to visit, people are often seeking a particular emotional state of mind. Some places make the mistake of trying to entice visitors with lists of their Chamber of Commerce members and images of the city's generic physical attributes. The feelings that prospective visitors desire are not captured in lists, attractions or businesses. These are the *features* of the place and rarely connect on an emotional level. The number one challenge for places is to connect with this desire to feel good (or better), because that's the ultimate hot button or trigger for all place-related decisions.

We only have to look at the growing popularity of spas, luxury resorts and places with celebrities to confirm the power of emotional benefits. Also note the influence of television programs and films in the increased awareness and esteem for some places. Recent television and films have placed the spotlight on the Jersey Shore NJ, Venice (Italy), and locations around Britain associated with Harry Potter. They may have always been popular destinations, but the heightened media attention gives them added cache and marks them as even more desirable places to be associated with.

Climb the Brand Value Pyramid

The brand benefits pyramid (Figure 3) demonstrates the importance of the brand to customers and the effect that emotional and social benefits have on them. All brand managers should aim to be associated with the qualities at the peak of the pyramid. Occupying this spot makes it difficult for other communities to succeed in offering the exact same value. Gaining this position could be called the Holy Grail for place branding because it is the ultimate positioning for those who want to rise above the many other places that are only relying on their physical attributes and features.

The closer to the peak of the triangle that the city climbs when delivering value through emotional benefits the more it will be differentiated and the more firmly it will bond with visitors in a way that will be extremely hard for others to match. A place engaged in a competitive tussle with another location should try to move up the pyramid by establishing an emotional benefit that the other place cannot easily deliver.

While emotional benefits start to appear on the third step of the pyramid, it is when they bond with the customer's personal values and beliefs at the pinnacle that they become their most potent. A person's motivation for visiting the city

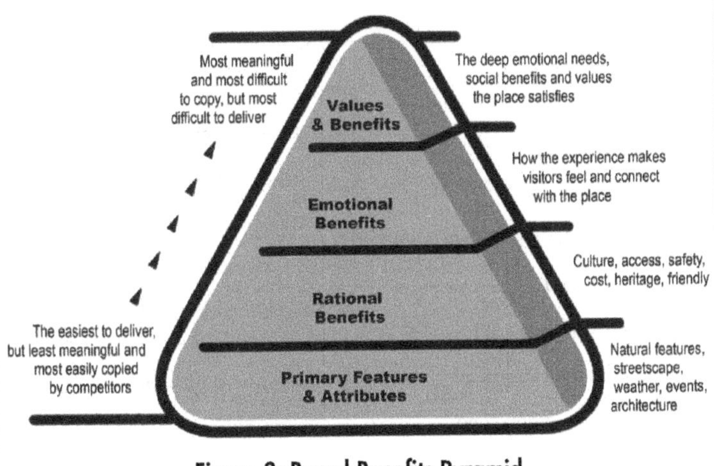

Figure 3: Brand Benefits Pyramid

is closely aligned with their personal values and beliefs or because it provides an important social benefit for them from being associated with the place. When cities occupy a spot at the peak, they enjoy greater loyalty and positive word of mouth than those on the lower levels of the pyramid. They are also likely to command higher prices and can usually generate more media coverage, investment, and goodwill than most of their competitors.

Seeing Things from The Customer's Perspective

The more that a city can learn about its customers by segmenting them according to their needs and desires, the better it is able to connect with them. Below are some of the deep-felt emotional connections on which cities can base their positioning, communications and experiences.

Whatever benefits are selected, they must provide a competitive edge. When two places share the same attributes, it is the emotional and social benefits that will be the tie breaker and provide the distinctive point of difference.

More and more destinations are responding to the trend for short breaks and the

- To attract the opposite (or same) sex
- To be entertained
- To be indulgent
- To be informed
- To be in style or fashionable
- To become more fit and healthy
- To challenge oneself
- To connect with people
- To escape (many things)
- To express love and romance
- To feel like a good parent
- To feel successful
- To feel pampered
- To feel superior or first
- To gain confidence
- To make a better world (volunteering)
- To pursue a passion
- To reward oneself

emotional reward of escaping everyday stress. Central to the brand identity of Palm Springs and Desert Resorts CA is escaping the worries and pace of everyday life, while Asheville NC invites people in nearby metropolitan areas to enjoy the city *any way you like it,* and the Eugene, Cascades and Coast region in Oregon offers Portland's residents the opportunity to escape the stresses of big city living for *Real Adventures. Real Close.*

Many coastal towns use their beaches as the point of differentiation. But all beaches are not the same. What does it feel like to escape a crowded city and sit under a palm tree on a deserted, white sand beach with just the sound of the gulls and the pounding surf? What emotions and sensations does it stimulate? Is this different to the experience and sensations on a beach lined with high-rise apartments, night clubs, music, and boutique shops? Should both places be communicating the same emotional and social benefits?

We often see the same imagery for all types of beach experience, missing the distinctive promise of how each place can make you feel and how it's different. The benefits from all coastal communities and beaches are not the same, as you can discover on a short drive along the California coast from the casual upscale escapes and "active relaxation" of San Diego North, to the inspiration of the artistic talent in Laguna Beach, to Santa Monica presenting "the essence of California lifestyle." Each is clearly differentiating itself, including offshore Catalina Island which invites us to escape to "the island of romance."

Creating the Destination Promise™

The Destination Promise™ is a series of carefully formulated statements that guide everything the place does when building its brand. When completed it is the Destination Promise™ and not the tagline that you follow. This is the foundation for all future steps and should have an influence on every marketing, organizational, invest-

The Destination Promise™ is the foundation for all future marketing programs and should have an influence on every marketing, organizational, and development decision.

ment and development decision (Figure 4). Its creation should not be rushed and every word must earn its place. Critical words should explode with meaning. The Destination Promise™ needs to be considered from both the customer's point of view, as well as from the perspective of residents, partners, and stakeholders. It outlines the key audience, tangible and emotional benefits, and states what sets it apart and why only this location is capable of satisfying the audience in this way. The Destination Promise™ is formulated after thorough analysis of the city's strengths from the demand perspective, i.e. considering the needs and wants of prospective customers and the supply perspective, i.e. the ability of the place to sustain their delivery.

Figure 4: The Destination Promise™ Informs all Programs

The Importance of the Destination Promise™

The basic tenet of a brand is that it is a promise that will be fulfilled. Our experience in building place and destination brands has shown us the need to move beyond the traditional positioning statement and create a precise promise that will lead its brand behavior. This evolved into what we call the Destination Promise™, articulating what the city wants to be known for, and what customers can expect.

Time and again, designing the Destination Promise™ in a collaborative and research-based manner has proven successful in helping stakeholders abandon self-interest and parochialism for more customer-centric thinking. It spells out how the place will remain relevant, competitive and compelling. Importantly, the Destination Promise™ acts as a reality check to ensure the place can fulfill its commitment. This concise statement sets the strategic language and roots for the future management of the brand. The following is an example of a Destination Promise™ for a fictitious place called Smithville, Colorado.

Smithville represents Colorado's foremost combination of mountain and cultural experiences. It has dramatic scenery, small town charm, spas, outstanding restaurants and a year-round cultural calendar. Only Smithville uniquely combines mountain tranquility, a thriving colony of renowned artists, and a national historic district with experiences that enrich, rejuvenate and provide spiritual satisfaction for visitors.

Testing the Promise

Once you have a draft of the Destination Promise™, it should be tested with stakeholders and ideally with customers as well. You are not looking for them to rewrite it, but to assess it for clarity, believability, and whether it captures the competitive identity of the place. If necessary, it can then be fine-tuned to enhance its relevance, appeal, and content.

The Promise should be evaluated in terms of its:

- Authenticity – Will prospects believe the underlying proposition?
- Differentiating – Will it really make the city stand apart in a way that is meaningful?
- Enduring – Is it deliverable and is it sustainable?
- Growth – Are there opportunities for product development, business growth and investment?
- Motivating – Is it an inspiring and enticing proposition?
- Relevant – Will it matter to a sufficient number of customers?
- Strategic – Does it fit with the vision, strategic objectives, and community values?

Questions

- What is the city's competitive advantage?
- What are the strengths, key benefits and core experiences?
- What are the components of the brand platform?
- What positioning should be claimed?
- What are the core experiences that underpin the Destination Promise™?
- Can we grow this proposition as an engine for economic development and investment?

CHAPTER TEN

Step Three: Architecture and Alignment – What Are the Brand's Relationships?

Brand architecture defines the relationships, structure and links that exist between a city brand's internal locations and partners, and how they fit in the wider geographical, thematic and marketing context. It relates to the synergy and advantages that can be achieved when they are seen as sharing strong common attributes that are in demand by target audiences.

Brand architecture is strongest when it unites places and leverages their common strengths, particularly those that are core elements of the brand.

Brand architecture is strongest when it unites places and leverages their common strengths, particularly those that are core elements of the brand. When defining the brand you must always be conscious of the relationships and alignment with other entities and places within, and outside, of the city and their roles in deploying the brand strategy. Ensure that there will be consistency and unity across these organizations before finalizing the brand platform. In regard to external brands that yours will be associated with, it's important that your common and strongest elements can be fully leveraged. For instance, if the city is known for its wineries, can this be leveraged with the strengths of regional and state brands?

I believe that the brand architecture model, when applied to places, departs somewhat from that which is normally ascribed to consumer goods. While there may be a difference, it's still important to consider the relationships, who they work with, and how other brands are often integral to their success. Places need a more hybrid brand architecture because they feature many permutations and audiences (tourism, economic development, investment, real estate and education) and all involve different relationships with other brands and places.

It's possible that customers might see the place as simultaneously linked or related to multiple other places, attractions or entities. Taking the high level view from space you will see that your city is part of your state and county brands, as well as your nation brand, and maybe it's also part of a themed destination brand such as a scenic route or special interests, e.g. The Revolutionary War battlefields or Monticello Wine Trail. It might also be connected to a variety of other place or destination brands within and outside of the city depending upon the audience and the aspects of the city's brand portfolio being offered. For tourism purposes, Cairns in Tropical North Queensland is externally part of Brand Queensland and Brand Australia. It is also an element in Australia's educational brand as well as its tourism and investment brands. Within Cairns and Tropical North Queensland (*the master or parent brand*), there are *sub-brands* such as the Great Barrier Reef, Port Douglas, Kuranda Village, Quicksilver Cruises, and many place marketing organizations that are integral to making Tropical North Queensland one of Australia's most magnetic brands.

The Origins of Brand Architecture for Places

The brand manager of consumer goods, when designing the brand architecture, is likely to be free to make or eliminate links to other products and organizations. In the case of places, there may be elements that cannot be eliminated because they are links and relationships that have developed organically through geography, history, politics, marketing and the media. However, brand managers can prioritize those relationships and links that will be most advantageous to all. Critical to the success of places is optimizing the "cards" they have been dealt.

The brand architecture of a particular city or region may be influenced by:

- Its objectives, competitive strengths and partners, i.e. is it an overarching place brand or is it focused only on tourism, economic development or community?
- Internal elements such as towns, downtowns and attractions that comprise the sub-brands.
- The external brands that give it meaning, coherence and attractiveness, such as a regional, state, national or a themed brand.

Internal Brand Architecture

When it comes to understanding the individual sub-brands or elements within a city or regional brand, the family metaphor is most appropriate. When we observe members of the family together we see that they are different and independent individuals. However, we also see a family resemblance in each of them because they share the family DNA. These relationships can add credibility (and disadvantages) in the marketplace. It is this commonality that creates the opportunity for individual sub-brands to benefit from the city, regional, state or nation brand if this shared DNA or brand essence can be leveraged and communicated in ways that are attractive to specific audiences. For example, within Portland OR are the sub-brands of Downtown, Pearl District, PDX Airport, the Columbia Gorge, and a host of other visitor attractions as well as the entities representing the city for economic development and investment. Portland also benefits from its external relationships with the Pacific Northwest, Oregon, the U.S.A, and the Oregon Trail.

External Brand Architecture

When marketing activities are conducted in distant locations where the city or region might not be well known, the brand can gain strength and context from its association with the better known national, state or regional brands. For example, when exhibiting at trade events in foreign countries, small cities as a general rule shouldn't go their own way, but work under the umbrella of their state or national brands. This provides valuable context, not to mention greater market leverage. Whereas in locations closer to home where there is greater familiarity with the city, it is much more important to exhibit independently in order to convey the distinctiveness of the place.

The objective is to develop a brand strategy that leverages relationships with other brands for greater awareness, distribution and penetration. But also know when it's best to go it alone. For example, for the marketing of the Napa Valley CA in Germany, it is important that it links itself to the American, Californian and San Francisco brands, but when marketing to audiences on the West Coast of the USA, it should be seen as a single destination or with San Francisco.

Brand Architecture in Action

The marketing materials of cities (particularly from government agencies), often coming from within the same building, can look as if they were produced by different cities. While the messages from these various agencies don't have to be identical (due to different audiences), it should be apparent that they are referring to the same place. When promoting the lifestyle and visitor strengths of the city, economic development marketers should project the city as prescribed in the brand strategy for tourism rather than making up their own descriptions, and vice versa.

Each of the city's marketing entities must employ messages that are fine-tuned to their particular audiences and, when appropriate, use common words, phrases, descriptions, images, colors and designs. Adopting these brand elements can prove far more effective than simply striving to create the same positioning, logo and tagline for all entities.

A place brand is not consumed in the same way as a consumer product. At times, even competitors must unite cooperatively to present a coherent, seamless experience to communicate and deliver the city's brand. This can be seen by visiting the booth for a city or region at a trade show. Here you will likely see fierce competitors collaborating to build better awareness and brand equity for their city's brand.

The brand architecture of a city may be based on its long-established geographical and marketing relationships with other places, and at the same time have an alternate architecture based on their involvement in a thematic brand. For example, Scotland's Castle Trail includes the popular destinations of Aberdeen, Braemar and Ballater. The challenge for small cities on the Trail is to optimize their relationships as an element of the thematic brand, however the greatest priority for Aberdeen is likely to be optimizing its strength as a stand-alone city brand.

Questions

- Will the proposed brand be in harmony across your city's marketing portfolio, e.g. economic development, tourism, recruitment? Does it need to be?
- Have you optimized links to potential sub-brands?
- Is the brand likely to be in harmony with regional, state and nation brands in meaningful ways?
- Are the partner's brand strategies compatible with yours?
- Are there shared values, goals and quality standards?
- Will the link open new markets and aid distribution?
- Will it give you access to improved exposure, technology, expertise and resources?

CHAPTER ELEVEN

Step Four: Articulate – How Will the Brand Be Expressed?

Now that you are armed with the brand platform and Destination Promise™, the focus moves to the design of the visual and verbal identity systems. The emphasis shifts from the left-brain logic that has driven the brand planning, to right-brain innovation and creativity which inspires the brand's designs and communications.

Prepare Creative Briefs

The first step is to relay the brand strategy to the creative team for the development of the tagline and to design the logo and other visual identity elements. The best method is through a concisely written creative brief and a series of conversations to ensure the team clearly understands the strategy and specific requirements. The brief is a tool that should inspire creativity and strategic alignment. It should outline the brand platform, target audiences, summary of competitor designs and those of partners within the city, and describe any legacy designs such as past logos, taglines, and industrial or cultural influences. It is also important to specify any colors, tone and feel, and references that should not be included in the identity.

The Brand Advisory Committee's Role

Committees have a pretty bad reputation in designing great art, poetry and symphonies. But the Brand Advisory Committee can play a valuable role in determining the visual and verbal identity, provided they don't micro-manage or try to re-design the logo or tagline themselves. From the outset it's important that the role and responsibilities of committee members be defined and that they understand the criteria for evaluating the various options that will be presented to them.

When logos are presented to a brand committee or city council meeting, some participants have a tendency to assume the mantle of design experts and allow their personal opinions, style, and preferences to overpower the need for objectivity and alignment with the brand strategy. This can happen despite their level of participation in the planning process to date. Simply because a committee member personally dislikes purple, or Garamond font, or anything with an art deco influence should not distract from the best work of experts in the design field. Worse still, animosities and politics can surface and get in the way. Those on the committee holding narrow views of branding can derail the project if they don't take a more holistic approach and consider the project as a whole and not just the logo (or tagline) they are reviewing.

Mary Klugherz, Principal at Great Destination Strategies correctly observes, "Branding professionals understand the principles of creating stunning designs and engaging words for taglines that are reflective of the brand and help distinguish it from competitors. Too often, however, the design process can get bogged down by committees trying to micro-manage graphic design decisions. This leads to too many compromises and often bland, uninspiring and generic results. Or worse, the logo contains everything in it but the kitchen sink leaving the community without a distinctly branded visual identity."

Logo and tagline approvals tend to absorb a disproportionate amount of attention and energy among branding committees and some local constituents.

If the committee (or locals) had to decide what color to paint the meeting room, there would not be 100% agreement on any one color. This is also to be expected when reviewing logos and taglines – you will probably never get 100% agreement, or even 80%. It is vital to avoid a negative spiral where the sides become entrenched with their own views and lose strategic focus. Their opinions must be balanced with the feedback from external customers.

Designing the Verbal Identity

The verbal identity includes the name, tagline, copy style, brand stories, and elements that make the brand's language distinctive, enticing, and informative. It is not uncommon for the power of words to be initially overlooked in favor of the colorful lure of the logo, yet words are among the most potent and affordable tools at your disposal. By consistently using carefully chosen words, phrases and stories that best support the identity, you can cost-effectively build the brand.

What's in the Name of a Place?

Glancing at a map of just about any country, it's easy to find places that are playing with a handicap. Names like Mousehole (Cornwall, England), Lick Skillet (VA) and Hairy Hill (Alberta, Canada) may bring a smile to your face. But others, such as Looneyville (TX and VA), Satan's Kingdom (Vermont), and Ugley (Essex, England) are names that could be a drawback for the town. Then there are names like Skaneateles NY and Skamokawa WA which can be difficult for non-locals to pronounce, let alone try to remember or spell.

The name of a place is the most powerful part of its identity. It has often been said that being introduced to a brand is like meeting a person. Their name is important – it's how we remember them, make associations, and refer to them. It's as if there is a filing cabinet in our brains where we keep everything relevant to that name. When we hear London, Paris or Saigon, we recall the many pieces of information, thoughts and feelings large and small, that we have assembled about each over the years, even if we have never been there.

The name of a place is the most powerful part of its identity. .... it's how we remember them, make associations, and refer to them.

On the other hand, if we hear Springfield TX, we have to be careful not to confuse it with the information we have stored about Springfield IL, Springfield OR, or Springfield MA. Hence, it is important – though not always possible – to have a name that is distinctive and not easily confused with others. In the USA, at last count there are 33 Washington counties, and more cities named Springfield than just about any other. Sometimes the city's name may not be ideal for marketing purposes, but impossible to change because of resident's emotional attachment to it. Unlike consumer brands that usually engage a naming specialist to research the most appropriate names for their products, cities already have names and many may have been used for centuries.

The names of places can change in recognition of local or national shifts such as newly won independence, nationalism, new political orientations or to highlight cultural influences. On the other hand, the change might occur to enable the city to compete more effectively. Over recent decades we've seen the Indian cities of Bombay, Calcutta and Madras become Mumbai, Kolkata and Chennai. Since 1994, a number of changes have been made to place names in South Africa, like Pietersburg, Louis Trichard, and Potgietersrust which became, Polokwane, Makhoda, and Mokopane.

Changing a city name can be a minefield and should be approached with great caution and transparency. There's no assurance that residents will readily endorse or approve a city name change, no matter the logic of your argument. While it's possible there will be economic development benefits, there is always the need to consider the costs for every organization in the city. What are the added marketing costs for local businesses, i.e. new advertising, collateral materials and websites? How long will it take for the new name to appear on official maps and signs? Is there likely to be a loss of brand equity in changing the current name? How long will it take before the new name gains traction?

There are many examples of places that have failed in attempting to change their official names. Residents often look at their city name differently than place marketers. First and foremost, every community is a place where residents may have lived all of their lives, where they went to school, married, had children, built their careers and operated businesses. The place and its name may have deep meaning and invoke strong passions because it is also a personal reflection of themselves, their social status, and their life choices. Their parents and grandparents may also share those same passions and the thought of changing the city name is hard for many to contemplate.

An example of this deeply rooted pride was shown by the citizens of White Settlement TX who voted in a ballot initiative to hold onto their heritage rather than change the city name to West Settlement. The city received its name in the 1840s when it was the lone village of white pioneers amid several American Indian encampments in the Fort Worth area of the Texas Republic. The initiative failed despite city leaders informing residents that the name was misleading and had deterred companies from moving into the area. [20]

In Oregon, the small town of Detroit wanted to differentiate itself from the auto-making city in Michigan. A proposal called for the name to be changed to Detroit Lake, the same as a nearby reservoir noted as a popular summer recreation site. It sounded like a great idea, but in a ballot measure the residents rejected the change. Similarly, a campaign to change the name of Commerce City CO to Victory Crossing fell flat. Conversely, in 1992 the city of East Detroit, Michigan changed its name to Eastpoint in an attempt to disassociate itself with neighboring, Detroit.

The name change was not so difficult for Sleepy Hollow, New York which changed its name from North Tarrytown in 1997 in honor of Washington Irving's famous short story *The Legend of Sleepy Hollow*. Residents had a deep sense of pride in the story which was associated with the area and thus made the name change somewhat easier.

In 1994, the citizens of St. Petersburg Beach FL voted to shorten the name to St. Pete Beach to lessen the confusion with the nearby city of St. Petersburg. Even with the name change it is frequently misspelled as St. Petes Beach, Saint Petersburg Beach or St. Petersburgh Beach. Nevertheless, St. Pete Beach has developed a strong identity and is widely supported by locals because it matched the way that residents colloquially referred to their city.

The lesson is that changing the official name of a place can be very contentious and controversial. It also highlights that while a name change might make sense from a brand image perspective, there is certainly no guarantee that residents are prepared to sever their emotional links with the current name. So tread with caution! Name changes demand thorough research, careful consideration and full support of residents – and even then the change is rarely a straightforward solution.

Is It Easier to Change the Destination Name?

While the prospect of changing the official name of a place may be extremely controversial and follow a political and bureaucratic process, there is usually much less debate attached to changing a destination name. A destination name is not necessarily the official name but might be created and used by tourism marketers to promote one or more contiguous places. The synergy from this approach can strengthen all participants more than if they marketed themselves individually. The destination name might not appear on official maps, or even Google Maps but serves to present the places in a meaningful way to prospective visitors and as such has the capacity to form its own brand identity.

There are many examples in the USA and other countries of destination names replacing county and even city names for tourism marketing purposes. This approach can make the name of the area more attuned to the needs and interests of prospective visitors. Some places, such as counties have been named for geographical necessity and political purposes, but the term "county" is rarely successful as an attractive destination name. Using a destination name enables places to develop a more appealing identity for tourism marketing. For example in Louisiana, St. Mary Parish rebranded itself as The Cajun Coast, in Florida the Emerald Coast stretches about 100 miles embracing many cities, and The Wild Coast was established on South Africa's Eastern Cape.

Lane County OR covers a large area (4,610 square miles) and embraces the Cascade Mountains, the McKenzie River Valley, stretches of the famed Oregon Coast, and parts of the Willamette Valley. Our research revealed that Lane County as a destination name was not strongly resonating with audiences despite more than a decade of marketing the county identity and despite the region's main city of Eugene being well known nationally. The name of the region was changed in 2009 to Eugene, Cascades & Coast with the goal of increasing awareness and marketability of its three well known sub-regions.

The Wilmington / Cape Fear CVB encountered resistance when proposing a name change for their region to *Wilmington. River District and Island Beaches.* It had previously been marketed as Cape Fear Coast. Officials representing beach communities wanted a name that more clearly identified individual towns. Interestingly, the change was not greeted enthusiastically by some visitors. While the individual city leaders may have had parochial interests, the visitors missed the appeal of Cape Fear because of the movies of that name – the original from 1962 and the remake in 1991, and the words Cape Fear also evoke a certain mysterious notion of a rugged coast.

What's the Lead Marketing Organization's Name?

The city or destination name is not the only name of significance to the branding and marketing of a place. In the corporate world the name of the corporation might be different to the name of its products. This is the case for Proctor & Gamble which makes

Tide, Pringles, Old Spice and dozens of other individually named products. In destination and place branding we can consider there to be a corporate name, i.e. the destination marketing organization (DMO) and a product name, i.e. the place name.

There's the need for an ongoing effort to build a brand identity for the lead organization or DMO itself with its constituents separate from, but related to, the destination brand. This is based on the concept of the organization being the official face and voice of the place for customers. The action should position the organization as objective, unbiased, and having no commercial agenda to its role as the "friendly concierge." This may also include making the CEO a high-profile spokesperson in and for the community. [21]

The naming of DMOs has been in an evolutionary phase for more than a decade as many transition to new names in an effort to better define their roles and relevance. Some are shedding names such as Convention & Visitors Bureau (CVB), Tourism Bureau and Visitors or Tourism Association. DMO names such as VisitNorfolk which replaces Norfolk CVB, San Francisco Travel replaces San Francisco CVB, and Travel Portland replaces Portland Oregon Visitors Association. Others are trying to project a more commercial identity such as NYC & Company, LA Inc. and Positively Cleveland.

Maura Gast, CEO of Irving TX CVB says, "Before any DMO sets off on the path of renaming itself (or repositioning or rebranding its corporate identity, for that matter), there needs to be a very clear goal of who the audience is that the name change is intended to serve. Whatever it is we call ourselves, the travel and tourism industry understands who we are and what we do. Where we need the positioning, the awareness, the identity – for the most part – is on the home front, in our respective political backyards and with our residents. This really isn't about whether or not "CVB" or "DMO" is the right word, phrase or fit. None of what we call ourselves, or logo on a street banner, matters if the audience we're trying to convince has no frame of reference for what we do."

Travel Lane County's Kari Westlund offers some interesting insights into the steps needed for a smooth destination or DMO name change. She says, "Be sure that your decision is based on input from stakeholders – local hospitality business leaders, policy leaders, residents, and your key customer groups. Don't expect to find a solution that has universal appeal, but strive for a decision that has broad support, is based on stakeholder input, and can be explained logically. Be sure to monitor results and maintain flexibility for incorporating small changes without losing your resolve for the change. Keep your process top of mind with key stakeholders and be prepared to repeatedly articulate why you made the change, how you decided on the new name, the benefits to local cities and businesses and how visitors are responding. Most importantly, keep your mission and responsibility in mind from start to finish. You are in business to create business."

Taglines, Slogans and Mottos

A tagline is a word or short phrase that captures the spirit of the Destination Promise™ and brand essence. The tagline can be a tease, a short descriptor, a call to action, or an explanation, and succinctly stated in no more than five words. You may choose to create one to support the destination or place name and logo, although this is not essential. That's right. A tagline is optional.

What's Starbucks tagline? They don't have one! Neither do Yakima Valley WA or Dunedin (New Zealand). They leave their communications and excellent experience delivery to convey who they are and what sets them apart. In keeping with Sheffield's (England) independent spirit, the city has not created a tagline – or a logo. If you choose to take this path, you must be sure that your partners and staff have a very clear understanding of the brand and how to deliver consistent and unified messages and experiences without the aid of these visual and verbal elements.

Sometimes a tagline is referred to as a slogan. However a slogan differs from a tagline in that a slogan is typically developed specifically for an advertising campaign and has a limited use. A tagline is created for indefinite use in a variety of applications. In England and a few other countries, a tagline or slogan might be referred to as a strapline.

Motto is a term that is sometimes used by the media and city officials. A motto is more about reminding stakeholders of some beliefs or ideals. Whenever I hear of a motto in relation to a place it just seems like the city believes it has a mantra for success – if they repeat it enough times! Usually, the phrase "Our motto is ..." is followed by a cringe-inducing line that has no link to any strategic intent or what may connect with external audiences.

According to urban economist Richard Florida, "Attaching a catchy slogan to a place doesn't work unless it captures something real, authentic, and evocative – and that's a whole lot harder than it looks. Many cities end up with clunkers. Plus, it can't just be a cute catch-phrase. It needs to reflect something unique or special the city has to offer." [22]

Periodically, some places come to the realization that their tagline is not a good ambassador for them and is outdated, boring and without meaning. They set out to replace it and mistakenly call this action "branding" when all they've done is taken a shortcut to a new design, one that soon becomes very lonely and meaningless. Whenever I see a tagline, I find myself asking: where did it come from? Was this simply a bright idea that somebody had, or is it connected to something deeper where the city has a strategic intent and is trying to address a specific objective? Too often, I fear that the former is the case. The tagline should promise or infer something that has meaningful benefits and can be valued by customers. It must be more than simply a clever line that carries no clear meaning, value or benefit. Great taglines are few and far between.

Some places come to the realization that their tagline is not a good ambassador for them and is outdated, boring and without meaning.

Being home to the Rock and Roll Hall of Fame was the catalyst for the Cleveland OH brand and their tagline *Cleveland Rocks!* Of course, the popular television program, The Drew Carey Show helped by starting and ending each episode with the cast dancing in the streets to the 1979 hit song Cleveland Rocks! All too rarely do we see a city tagline that is capable of carrying a brand. This one was bang on target!

Too many destination taglines are simply examples of marketing speak or clichés that do nothing to advance the identity of the place. Another pitfall worth considering is ending up with a tagline that is so esoteric that it needs extensive (and expensive) marketing communications to convey its meaning.

Few small cities have the marketing budgets to communicate the meaning and relevance of their taglines through advertising. Wherever appropriate, I like straightforward, descriptive taglines for small cities because, if done correctly, they never stop working and don't need other marketing communications to explain their meaning. Examples of these are Oshkosh *Wisconsin's Event City*, Fredericksburg TX, *German Heritage. Texan Hospitality* and Austin TX, *Live Music Capital of the World*. Descriptive taglines speak directly, clearly state what they are about and single out what differentiates them from other choices. They're probably not "sexy," but they earn their keep – especially if you have a small budget. Their drawback is that they may not always work for an overarching place brand.

Max Nofziger, a former Austin city council member who voted on the *Live Music Capital of the World* tagline back in 1991, comments: "I'm amazed that this is still a slogan of the city. I'm shocked it hasn't been repealed, frankly," he said jokingly, during the recent twentieth anniversary celebration of the brand. [23] I must share his amazement because one of the greatest hazards for city brands is the temptation for new councilors, employees and executives to adopt something new so that they can put their own stamp on it.

I like the perspectives of destination branding specialist, Tom Buncle from Yellow Railroad based in Edinburgh, Scotland. "Taglines are brilliant when they are inspired, convey a destination's benefits succinctly in a way that evokes the essence of the place, and could be nowhere else. It helps too if they say something new to you and say it in a way that grabs you, make you smile or think "yeah, that's nicely put," i.e. impactful, memorable, and usually containing one strong idea. But mostly they fail spectacularly. And how much money has been wasted with expensive agencies generating mediocre calls to action in insipid taglines?"

Buncle adds, "The risk is that a destination looks amateurish and hick if it tries too hard and fails to come up with a compelling tagline – in which case no tagline at all is better than an embarrassingly lame one that patronizes consumers – and residents. If you can't come up with the Holy Grail of a killer tagline, use a descriptive one or one that anchors the place in a single powerful idea, e.g. Angus: *Scotland's Birthplace* or Innsbruck: *Capital of the Alps* which at least paints a picture of your destination, or be brave and don't have one. In other words trust your product, get your brand and marketing right, and treat consumers as potential visitors who want to be inspired and informed, but not patronized."

Many words and terms used in taglines are so over-used or misused that they've lost their potency. They are like wallpaper – people have seen them so often that they take very little notice of them and place them into the realm of "advertising-speak." Others are devalued because the customer suspects that the proposition is an exaggeration or simply cannot be true. Lines such as "the best of," "we've got it all," "best kept secret," "friendliest place" and "warm welcome" are usually not credible and are considered inane and patronizing. Other words that are in risk of being over-used include nature, natural, explore, discover, and friendly and perhaps the worst of all, a great place to live, work and play.

This checklist includes eight filters that may be helpful as you evaluate your proposed tagline:

- It captures and dramatizes the Destination Promise™
- It is ownable and not the same or similar to other places
- It hints at a reward or benefit that customers value and can expect
- It's credible and sustainable
- It's short, usually less than five words
- It works with and enhances the logo
- It's easy to remember
- It does not have negative connotations

It's essential to check with the United States Trademark and Patents Office (www.uspoto.gov) to assess the availability of specific terms. Their site enables you to conduct a preliminary search for phrases and words that may already be trademarked and in use. We also recommend extensive online searches to assess whether the tagline is already in use or registered. As soon as your Brand Advisory Committee officially endorses the tagline, immediately register it as a trademark.

Key Words and Phrases

Just as the term "talking points" has found its way into our vocabulary to describe the words, phrases, and sentences that politicians consistently use to get their messages across, each city also needs its own talking points or key messages. Key words enable us to verbally communicate the brand in ways that consistently capture the distinctive essence of the place. This helps keep all staff, partners, and stakeholders "on message" when speaking or writing about the city. These words and phrases should always appear in all appropriate brochures, websites, speeches, and presentations. The brand's key words may differ from the key words used in search engine optimization which relate more to the terms that people use when searching for specific information.

Brand Stories

Since people first sat around a fire and recounted their hunting expeditions, stories have been used as a means of entertainment, instruction, and communication. Today, by tapping into the power of storytelling, brand managers can inject greater meaning and emotion into their brands. Brand managers can learn a lot from the words of famed attorney Gerry Spence who maintains "winning is just a matter of finding the right story." He frequently starts his courtroom summation with, "Now, let me tell you a story."

The stories, anecdotes, legends, and myths that are associated with a place make it all the more engaging and meaningful. The best brand stories recall and reinforce the brand essence of the place and can be the catalyst for deeper emotional connections. Depending on the audience they can be designed to be informative, inspirational or motivational.

Of course, some places have better and more engaging stories than others. Some are larger than life. Imagine the tales that the streets of Tombstone AZ tell about Wyatt Earp, or the Maori legends in Rotorua (New Zealand), or the Night Watchman's stories in medieval Rothenberg (Germany).

Wherever possible, brand stories should be woven into communications and experiences. They may relate to your brand credentials, which you identified as the "reasons to believe" in Step Two. All cities have their own stories and the most engaging are usually based on events, achievements, humorous happenings and interesting people. For example the origin of the Ford Motor Company in Dearborn MI, the folktales and legends of Bergen (Norway) or the buildings designed by world-famous architects in Rotterdam (The Netherlands). Some are unique to one place, while some, like the Underground Railroad, The Oregon Trail, or Scotland's Whiskey Trail are shared with several cities and regions.

Cities have the ability to bring their themes or stories to life throughout the destination experience. Whether standing in a place made famous by a city's favorite son, marveling at his achievements in the museum, walking a street named for him, or listening to a guide who knew him, most cities have abundant opportunities to tell their stories. Simply walking around some places can make you feel as though you are part of the story. Walking into an encampment of Civil War re-enactors near Gettysburg PA will make you feel as though you are "inside" some of the stories that defined the community (and the nation). When stories truly engage visitors, they are a powerful force for delivering outstanding brand experiences.

Interesting stories that engage prospective customers can make all the difference if a community is similar to competitors on other dimensions. Selma AL has been able to tell the inspiring stories of its involvement in the Civil Rights Movement to set it apart. Visitors to the city's National Voting Rights Museum can hear the first-hand accounts of guides who are veterans of the civil rights movement.

While several entrepreneurs have created "Magical Mystery Tours" of Beatles sites in Liverpool, wouldn't you rather experience a tour of the city designed by a Beatle? Sir Paul McCartney has announced that he'll design a sightseeing tour of his favorite paths and places throughout the city and the stories to go with them. Sir Paul said, "I have my own magical mystery tours of the city, my own special route I go on, and I think other people would love it too." [24] I think that's an understatement! This one-of-a-kind tour will certainly add to the celebrity and the authenticity of the Liverpool experience.

Design the Visual Identity

The visual identity system includes the logo, logotype, fonts, color palette, photo images, symbols, and the distinctive look or designs that express and represent the brand. It may also include the designs for special applications such as buildings, office interiors, furnishings, vehicles, uniforms, merchandise, street banners, signage, trade show booths, and more.

Logo

Logos comprise custom-lettered words, symbols, illustrations, emblems, or a combination of these elements. They are sometimes referred to as marks or brand signatures and include logo marks (graphic symbols), logotype (combines the graphic symbol and name in a specific arrangement) and word marks (comprising a typographic style and featuring the name and not the graphic symbol). After consistent use over time the logo should act as a trigger or cue to aid recall of the positive associations that the place is known for. Too frequently, the power and role of a logo is over-emphasized. Nobody will respond positively to a logo and then decide to visit a place if they haven't also been exposed to other compelling stimuli about the place.

Logos are faced with more challenges today than they were a decade ago. The wide use of mobile apps and other digital uses often require logos to be compressed for use on small screens. An added challenge for place logos in our globalized society is that they transcend cultural, national, and linguistic barriers. It is an arena in which simplicity works best. A complicated design will make a logo difficult to reproduce and maintain, and will most likely fail to engage the audience. Rather than adding complex elements, consider instead that less can be more powerful. Think of the shell in Shell's logo or the Nike swoosh or even the heart in I Love NY.

We have all seen those logos where a city has tried to cram everything into the design in an attempt to please all stakeholders. This was often the situation with city shields or crests when there was a belief that every city attribute had to be represented. A logo is not intended to be an advertisement. Due to the complexity of a place, a logo can rarely provide a summation of all of its elements. If tried, the result can be a confusing collage of features that are unrecognizable and are rendered meaningless, particularly when reduced in size. One of the challenges is to balance simplicity without being seen as boring or unimaginative.

Another mistake some cities make is conducting a competition among residents and students to design their new logo. The old adage, "be careful what you wish for because you might get it" comes to mind when looking at the competition winners for some cities. After conducting the competition for a tagline or logo they find themselves with designs that may be nice, but are unrelated to the city's competitive identity or the benefits that customers are seeking. A competition may be free or cheap, but believe me, places following this approach usually get what they pay for.

Fort Collins CO went through a difficult launch of their logo following the release of their brand strategy. Public criticism erupted around the new logo which replaced the city logo designed in 1974. There were many misunderstandings and incorrect information which resulted in overwhelmingly negative feedback from the public. The City Manager halted implementation and sought public input to find a solution. A local firm was hired to design an alternate logo which would be a balance between the outdated logo and the new, but rejected design. Residents were invited to vote for one of the three designs, including the old logo. The results were split evenly between the three designs, but the community made few complaints when the redesigned version by the local agency was designated the winner. This was a rare situation where some in the community were resistant to any sort of change. An approach such as this where the community selects the logo (or tagline) is not recommended because it can become a beauty pageant for internal stakeholders and loses strategic focus on the external customers.

Logos rarely stand in isolation. When evaluating prospective logos it is important to consider the context in which the design will be used and how it will be linked to images and text about the city. The most impactful and enduring designs are often those that feature a striking, singular symbol.

Despite having worked on logo designs for many months, the recommended design may not always be greeted enthusiastically when it is first revealed. Don't be dispirited. Customers, and stakeholders for that matter, don't always immediately understand the meaning of a design. Even the citizens of the USA didn't immediately grasp the meaning of the nation's flag, the Stars and Stripes, when it was first introduced. Betsy Ross simply created an interesting design featuring stars on a piece of fabric. It took many more years of tumult and triumphs to build its meaning, and relevance in the hearts of Americans. Logos can face similar challenges. They need time to connect, gain meaning and resonate.

Some of the criteria to use when selecting a logo are:

- Does it capture and dramatize the Destination Promise™?
- Does it have strong design qualities?
- Is it original and attractive?
- Is it simple and uncluttered?
- Can it be reduced for small-scale applications?
- Will it reproduce well in black and white?
- Is it suitable for use on merchandise and different mediums, i.e. electronic, glass, fabric?

To aid in final refinement and selection, test your three or four leading designs on prospective customers outside of the city. After the logo is selected, register it with the United States Trademarks and Patents Office.

Logotype

This is the typeface used in the logo or mark. It may comprise only the name of the place rather than a symbol. The logotype may use an existing, commonly available font which can be altered slightly for a more tailored look, or it may be a design featuring customized calligraphy. A custom illustrated mark will be more costly than one developed from an existing font.

Color Palette

How would you feel walking onto an aircraft with a black interior? How do you react when you see a billboard with a red background? Colors have a profound effect on our emotions and preferences. The selection of a color palette is an integral, yet under-utilized source of differentiation. Different colors carry different meanings. They may include:

Black	Power, dignity, serious, tradition, funereal
Blue	Tranquility, healing, knowledge, integrity, power
Brown	History, earthy, traditional
Green	Nature, health, freshness, calm
Pink	Feminine, soft, youthful
Red	Passion, aggressive, strength, vitality, stop
Turquoise	Calm, relaxation, soothing
White	Pure, clean, refined, truthful
Yellow	Fun, caution, youthful, sunshine, cowardly

When deciding on your color palette, avoid the dominant color used by your competitors. Are there colors that are indigenous to the area? Astoria-Warrenton OR is using a color pallet inspired by the labels for the salmon cans used by the old seafood canneries which once populated its shores.

Fonts and Typography

Your selection of fonts and typography may be subtle, but they make a strong statement. Just think of the hundreds of places where your written words will be seen. Beyond the logo, brochures and advertising, the look of your carefully chosen words have a powerful influence in everything from stationery and web pages to posters, name badges, and wayfinding signs.

Photography

High quality photography can be one of the most potent and versatile elements in your brand toolkit, yet most communities under-invest in it. It doesn't make sense to pay for advertising, printing and websites only to use inferior and off-brand images. Instead, present the city's distinctiveness, benefits, and personality through outstanding photography. Just as the consistent use of the logo builds the brand, so do high quality images that express core brand elements.

Questions

- Is the place name attractive and easy to remember?
- Have you identified key words, phrases and stories to express the brand?
- Do designs capture the Destination Promise™?
- Do the city logo and tagline have legal protection?
- Are the combined colors, fonts, and designs distinctive?
- Do your photo images support the Destination Promise™?

CHAPTER TWELVE

Step Five: Activation – How Will the Brand Come to Life?

It's now time to orchestrate the communications and on-brand actions that will elicit the desired responses from customers. There are many publications on the subjects of advertising, social media, public relations, Internet marketing, and brochure production so I will not go into any depth about them here. The focus in this chapter is to pinpoint how to activate and embed the brand identity into these applications.

Develop Creative Briefs

Producing clear guidelines and briefs is the best way to ensure that the brand is accurately and creatively represented by agencies and designers in all communications. It is particularly important when many partners and vendors are also communicating the brand.

One way to check that all brand communications are customer-focused and convey enticing benefits is to imagine that the customer is looking over your shoulder as you prepare the materials. Whenever possible, all communications should be led by core benefits and experiences and not littered with facts, member lists and information included only to please internal stakeholders. Marketing applications must answer the customer's perennial question, *"What's in it for me?"*

Remember, the most powerful, meaningful and appropriate benefits – the emotional rewards – should always be at the forefront.

Avoid talking about the city as a series of locations, attractions, and things to see and do. Instead, bring it to life as an experience and make customers feel as though they are already there sensing and feeling it whenever they read, see, or hear your communications. Make it easy for people to see themselves in the picture. And don't try to balance the images for political harmony. The customer doesn't care! Additionally, just as you would invest in the best graphic designer you can afford, invest in the best copywriter you can afford as well.

Brand Communications

Integrating your marketing messages is the most effective way to generate the most impactful communications. In a nutshell, this involves carefully synchronizing all advertising, public relations, web marketing, collateral, direct mail, and other communications. By orchestrating your communications in this way, you will generate synergy across all applications and expose customers to multiple, frequent and consistent brand images and messages, all the while maximizing the return on investment. While you may think that integrated marketing is the domain of places with large budgets, it is equally incumbent upon those with small budgets to synchronize their efforts in order to maximize their impact and effectiveness. Integrated communications can be even more effective when key partners in the community become part of the coordinated effort. The objective is to generate synergy across all applications irrespective of size.

So much leisure travel advertising by small cities is wasted because little of it adds to the knowledge and meaning that prospective customers have of the place. This is not to say that advertising is useless, it's that their small advertising budgets and their limited reach and frequency combined with the use of inappropriate and inconsistent messages often render their advertising largely ineffective.

Many destinations feel that if they could only produce really great advertising and have a mountain of money to buy media, they'd be able to build a successful brand. Unfortunately, they can't muscle their way into the modern consumer's mind like that. Brute force marketing that attempts to interrupt customers during their television watching, driving or reading is nowhere near as effective or efficient as it used to be.

Those places with the biggest advertising budgets and the most creative advertising don't necessarily win.

Today's customers place low trust in advertising, and that includes travel and tourism advertising. These are empowered consumers who are likely to be savvy and discerning. Prospective customers have access to peer review websites such as tripadvisor.com where they can review the opinions of past visitors to destinations, attractors and lodging to verify that a destination or hotel is really suitable for them.

Advertising

Advertising, whether print, broadcast or online, should always capture and dramatize the essence of the Destination Promise™. It should also consistently leverage the brand personality and benefits to ensure that they are strongly associated with the city. Wherever possible, advertising should observe the following branding rules of thumb:

- The city name, logo and tagline are prominently displayed.
- The copy and designs are true to the brand strategy.
- Don't try to tell the whole story – leave that up to the website, brochure or other communications.
- Encourage the consumer to take the next step.

Web Marketing

The city's website should be the central hub for all marketing and communications programs, as shown in Figure 5. It should provide the focal point for consumers, media, and partners to easily access information, advertising responses, enquiries, and interactive experiences. It is the most important and cost effective vehicle for expressing the brand. However, in order to achieve this, the website, like other marketing applications, must consistently adhere to the brand usage guidelines. The following are some brand-building rules of thumb that should be applied:

- The website projects both tangible and emotional benefits.
- It provides the "What's in it for me?" answer.
- It has a focus on key experience themes.
- The design and content conform to the brand guidelines.
- Database marketing principles are being applied.

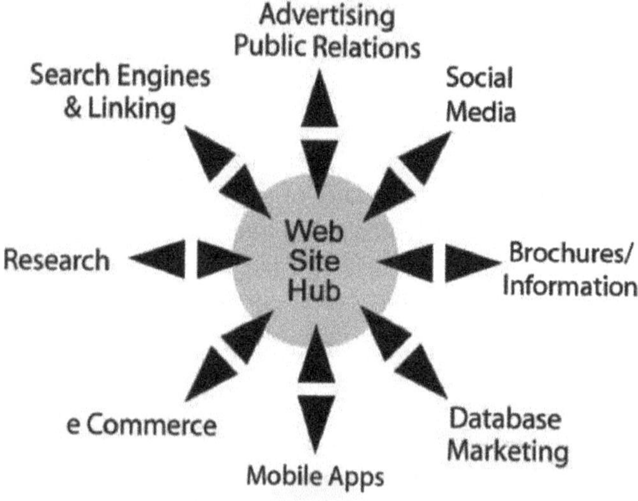

Figure 5: Web-based Integrated Marketing

Social Media and Word of Mouth

Your customers have never had more power. They have connectivity through ever-broadening digital platforms, from smartphones, tablets, email, and social media websites to instantly reach friends and family around the world – and while they are visiting your city.

Friends and relatives, past visits, customer comments on social media sites, and the independent advice of travel websites and guidebooks are highly influential in approximately 80% of travel decisions. I refer to these influences as experience-based or loyalty-based decisions because they have been heavily influenced by the loyalty and past experiences of customers.

It's still word-of-mouth that is the most powerful, and technology is amplifying the impact of this highly influential form of communication.

Traditional advertising and promotions may have then provided the stimulus for only 10%-15% of visitors. The customer's decisions based on these marketing applications could be regarded as "leap of faith" decisions because they call on the prospective visitor to make their decision based on trust in what they see and hear in marketing communications.

Despite all of the marketing media used today, it's still word-of-mouth that is the most powerful, and technology is amplifying the impact of this highly influential form of communication. Websites specializing in peer reviews, such as IgoUgo, Trip Advisor, and My Travel Guide are favorites among travelers who use the comments of past visitors to influence their travel decisions. This consumer generated content underscores the point that your brand is not what you say you are, but what your customers say you are. The challenge for destination marketers in this environment is to influence on-brand experiences at critical points of contact with visitors and to constantly monitor this content.

Quite clearly, it is important that city marketers address both the experience-based as well as the leap of faith-based influences to build their brand. In too many cases the focus is predominantly on the leap of faith-based generators with little or no attention being paid to producing word-of-mouth advocates through outstanding visitor experiences. This does not mean that I regard advertising and other paid leap of faith marketing activities as being of little or no value in building a brand. What I am suggesting is maintaining a holistic view of place branding that takes into account the total destination experience. Communities are often too quick to search for new prospects before they have capitalized on the opportunities that might be right in front of them – the low hanging fruit that is easiest to harvest. The most accessible advocates for positive word-of-mouth are current and past customers, employees, and residents.

An excellent example of the power of staff in influencing future visitation comes from the Main Street Associations in Virginia. Time and again, their surveys have shown that the most effective way to promote monthly events in each community was not through advertising, but by encouraging front line staff to personally invite customers to return for events. For instance when chatting to customers, they simply ask, "Are you coming along to First Thursday this week?" This simple, friendly question creates the opportunity to promote an event and extend a personal invitation. Similar success in positively influencing customer behavior can be seen in the actions of enthusiastic staff in information centers, attractions, lodging, and restaurants around the country. This is a reminder of the potential power that your front line staff have in projecting your brand, both correctly and incorrectly.

Mobile Technology

Mobile technology brings with it new challenges for projecting a brand through the small space of a smartphone or tablet screen. In addition to web surfing, customers have access to mobile sites such as Google Maps, or location-based social networking sites like Foursquare and place specific apps such as those developed for specific locales, attractions and other leisure sites. These are tools with great potential for place branding and marketing but will require constant attention to the rapidly evolving technologies and branded apps. They are enhancements for your information distribution systems, but at this stage they are not replacements for current elements.

John Hope Johnstone from HPR Internet & Social Media Marketing sees the importance of mobile platforms. He says, "These are key for converting interest into actual bookings. While mobile services are still emerging in the marketing of cities, it is apparent that visitors are clearly beginning to expect, demand and adopt them with 16% of travelers surveyed currently using smartphones to book trips, according to an Amadeus Report entitled "The Always-Connected Traveler" [25] That figure rises to 18% amongst the 18-35 year olds and to 33% amongst frequent travelers. 84% of survey respondents said it is important to offer a program that allows travelers to book elements of their itinerary using mobile devices. The message for cities is quite clear. Mobile is rapidly expanding and they must ensure that their mobile platform is integral to their communications strategies."

Video and Sound

Advances in technology, and specifically the Internet, have created vast opportunities for using video and sound in communicating brands. They are capable of reaching and engaging audiences, whether for TV programming, videos, advertising, or online marketing. The use of streaming video and sound tracks are powerful ways to increase brand awareness and present key messages. Cleverly produced videos by places, their visitors and residents can quickly go viral and generate millions of views on video sharing sites such as YouTube, Yahoo Video and Flickr. Their creative use should be integral elements in your brand activation.

Newport Beach CA has taken an interesting approach by sponsoring an internet radio play called Rockin' California, with the promotion line 'Fall in love with Newport ... And Listen Loud.' For the most part, it's a playlist of songs that make you feel like you're having fun on the beach or cruisin' the Pacific Coast Highway in a Corvette with the top down.

Public Relations

Why is it that some places seem to be featured more in the media than others? It's not by accident – more than likely the city is very media-savvy. Public relations play a valuable role in brand development and enhancing the reputation of the place. Every city should maintain a proactive public relations program irrespective of the size of its budget. PR is essential for any place wishing to enhance its attractiveness and reputation, and protect its good name. The most common elements in the marketer's PR toolkit are media releases, press kits, media visits, media conferences and briefings, promotions, bids, speeches and sponsorship.

Consumers are more likely to be engaged by, and indeed trust, a first-hand account by a trusted source than from paid advertising.

Strong public relations can be highly cost effective and, when executed well, generates increased visibility, awareness, and interest at a fraction of the cost of paid advertising. Whenever they appear in print, online, radio or on television, third-party articles and features have an enormous ability to inform and motivate. The benefits extend beyond tourism to projecting the city as an attractive place to do business and live. Consumers are more likely to be engaged by, and indeed trust, a first-hand account by a trusted source than from paid advertising.

The following is a checklist to consider when embedding brand messages:

- Do communications reflect the tone and personality of the brand?
- Does the press kit feature the visual identity and links to more detailed information and images?
- Develop three to five key messages that convey the essence of the brand in sound bites for speeches and presentations, and several key phrases to be used in written communications.
- Incorporate at least one key attribute and one emotional benefit in all written and spoken communications.

- Ensure spokepersons integrate those key messages into communications with the media and key clients.
- Track the coverage of key messages in articles, speeches, TV and radio interviews. If they're not being picked-up by the media, analyze why and revise their use accordingly.
- Keep in mind that this is not a one-time endeavor. Repetition is essential to build awareness and preference.

Brochures and Publications

Despite the advances in online communications, brochures continue to play an important role in marketing and visitor satisfaction. However, extreme care should be taken to ensure that they are well designed, thoughtfully written, and carefully distributed. Many cities waste far too much of their budget on brochures and their distribution.

We tend to be led by our emotions and then verify with our logic. The same applies when we make our travel decisions and purchases. Many cities try to promote themselves by using uninteresting lists of local attractions, businesses and services. While this information does have a role later in the decision-making of customers, it is rarely important at an early stage when visitors are developing their initial awareness and image of a destination. Lists of "what to see & do," "where to eat," and "where to stay" alone don't make emotional connections. Prospective visitors first need to be convinced of what is appealing and special about the place. To maintain maximum alignment with the brand, brochures should:

- Reflect the Destination Promise™ on the cover.
- Prominently feature the core experiences and benefits.
- Carefully follow the brand guidelines in regard to typography, logo use, color pallet, and design standards.
- Include copy that is based on the key words, benefits, phrases, and brand stories.
- Clearly demonstrate and address "*What's in it for me?*"

Delivering Brand Experiences

"Our brand is a living entity – and it is enriched or undermined cumulatively over time, the product of thousands of small gestures."

Michael Eisner
Former CEO, Disney

I particularly like the way in which Disney's former CEO Michael Eisner referred to the Disney brand when he said, "Our brand is a living entity – and it is enriched or undermined cumulatively over time, the product of thousands of small gestures." Delivering outstanding brand experiences through these gestures across a city or region calls for different types of partnerships and involvement with the most appropriate and influential people.

For a city or region to be truly differentiated in the customer's mind, it must focus on and expand the experiences that make it special. It is through the development and enhancement of these competitive, unique experiences that you able to connect with today's customer.

Tourism Australia's Regional General Manager UK / Europe Rodney Harrex highlighted the priority that Australia places on experiential branding when he said, "The success of Brand Australia is not conveyed by our advertising alone, but through all encounters and experiences with Australia and its people. To achieve this we are transforming the brand from being presented as a trip, vacation or destination to becoming a wholly immersive, aspirational and engaging experience."

How will you ensure that your Destination Promise™ is optimized at every critical touchpoint? Malcolm Allan, of Colliers International suggests that this can be difficult for places to achieve. "Obviously, not every single action, policy, investment or event of the city will be fully 'on brand' and some of them will even likely be 'off brand.' It is important that the key stakeholders realize and identify which of the multitude of their activities have significant impact on the brand that they wish to realize and manage and market them as a priority."

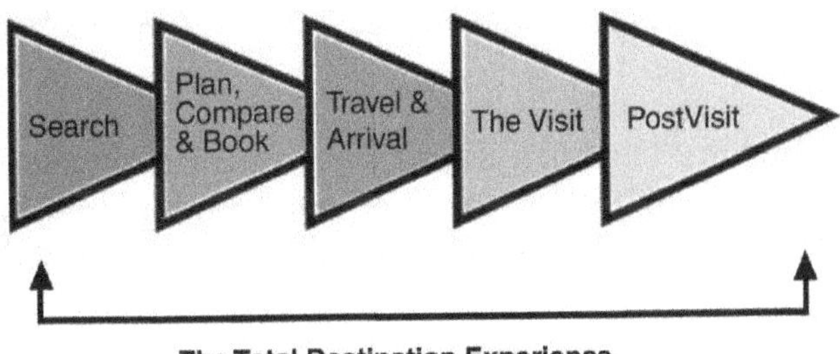

Figure 6: Total Destination Experience Model

This can be addressed through experience mapping, a concept that demonstrates how customers encounter the place by tracing the five stages in their experience. It reflects how customers proceed from one stage to the next, and their behavior, desires, and needs change. Variations on this model can be created for relocation and investment. The five stages of the total destination experience are:

1) Search: These early touchpoints influence whether the person becomes a customer for the place or not. Touchpoints include marketing communications, word of mouth, and past experiences.

2) Plan, Compare and Book: The touchpoints here commonly include fulfilling the questions from prospects and the ease of making transactions and bookings. They may relate to websites, reservations, price, incentives, conditions, packages, and staff.

3) Travel and Arrival: At this point the experience is well underway. The cost, quality, and ease of access and transport can influence attitudes. Upon arrival, is it easy to find your way around? What are the first impressions?

4) The Visit: During this phase customers are most conscious of the experiences associated with the place. What is the quality of the attractions and experiences? How are customers interacting with the place? What are the standards? What apps are available? What is the quality of signage, brochures, tour guides, taxi drivers, mobile apps and public spaces?

5) Post Visit: This phase doesn't often receive the attention that it deserves to build positive word of mouth and positive memories. What is role of surveys, social media sites, souvenirs and local products?

Phil Bruno from *Treat 'em Right* highlights the importance of on-brand experiences, "In our current recessionary economy, if your brand promise is not kept, you're in trouble. In other words, if you are saying that you are one thing and the guests find another to be true, you're toast! Since the recession began consumers are placing more emphasis on the value of their time and money equally. The pressure to deliver exactly (or even more than) what was promised has been elevated. It is essential that communities be vigilant at their key delivery points to ensure that they are all in tune with the brand promise. This involves educating all employees about the brand, expectations, and their role in delivering not only what's expected but maybe even a little bit, or a lot more."

Product Development and Placemaking

Product, service and experience delivery are frequently missing from place branding strategies, however their inclusion is essential to ensure that the city remains relevant and competitive. They are also the foundation for establishing and expanding small businesses. Experience delivery for relocation markets might be as simple as business-friendly approval systems and favorable zoning, while for tourism it may be far more complex involving government, private and non-profit organizations. Brand managers have a vital role in ensuring that the city's core experiences outlined in the Brand Platform are consistently delivered and remain fresh. There must be no gaps between expectations and the city's reality.

There are two types of experiences that are priorities to develop, manage and monitor. The first are the *core brand experiences.* These are the encounters that are essential to the experiential themes or clusters that underpin the Destination Promise™. The second are the touchpoints that are crucial throughout the total destination experience. The brand experience themes are likely to be centered on the main attractors, while touchpoints potentially involve almost any aspect of the place, including individuals and organizations outside of the city such as tour operators and media.

Product Development

This is the process by which new products, services and experiences are introduced and existing ones are improved. These actions are essential to the brand's sustainability, particularly a destination brand, and are a valuable conduit for increased profitability, job creation and investment. Product development initiatives might include:

- Capital investments in hotels, attractors and infrastructure
- Events, festivals, tournaments and exhibitions
- Improvements such as trails, parks, and boardwalks
- Packaging and bundling of products, and experiences
- Service and quality improvement programs
- Placemaking in the form of streetscapes, gateways, public art, and public spaces
- Thematic interpretation

It helps to consider places as experiential products. The following are examples of how some places are bringing their brands to life and creatively addressing the challenges of delivering on their promise.

Walking into the Visitor Information Center in Jackson WY the visitor immediately gets a sense of the region's personality and essence through large colorful displays, natural history exhibits, interactive sources of information, a quality souvenir and book store, and an observation deck from where you can watch elk grazing in the shadows of the spectacular Grand Tetons.

Many cities that establish their brand on a cultural attribute often have difficulty sustaining it. An exception is Austin TX. Having based its brand on being the "*Live Music Capital of the World*," it has kept this lofty positioning for two decades. What distinguishes Austin is that they didn't rest on their laurels, instead they continued to live the brand and keep it fresh. The positioning was based on Austin having more live music venues per capita than any other city in the country, including New York, New Orleans and Nashville. The city has grown in 20 years to include 250 live music venues featuring 50,000 live music performances every year.

The Paducah KY brand is centered on the city being '*distinctively creative*.' At a time when funding for the arts is being cut, Paducah fosters an environment where artists and the arts can flourish. Their Artist Relocation Program began in 2000 and while the financial incentives were limited to dilapidated housing in the downtown neighborhood at little cost (often as low as $1) and professional assistance of up to $2,500, the intrigue of becoming a member of a true art enclave proved irresistible. To date, seventy artists/residents have invested over $30 million in enhancing the historically hip character of downtown. What has emerged is a model for how struggling cities can reinvent themselves as a vibrant cultural and artistic enclave. And along the way they are continuously reinvigorating their brand. [26]

Huntington Beach CA is constantly working to sustain its reputation as '*Surf City USA*™.' The city has a distinct ambience based on its authentic surfing culture, which has been part of the fabric of the city for half a century, and is now the epicenter for a new generation of surf enthusiasts. In addition to hosting the biggest surfing event in the world, visitors are immersed in the surfing culture through the International Surfing Museum, the Surf Walk of Fame, and the Surfing Hall of Fame. As if this isn't enough, the city allowed the surfwear retailer Hollister to install web cams on the Huntington Beach Pier to transmit live images of the shoreline into fifty of its classic cabana-like stores nationwide.

The Shaoxing (China) brand *Vintage China* conducted an event named *25@100% Vintage Shaoxing Experiences.* The brand inspired a range of experiences within the event especially for the Shanghai expat market. These experiences were created to allow participants to immerse themselves in Shaoxing culture and the daily lifestyles of local people. The encounters included the opportunity to be an opera apprentice, cook at a popular restaurant, dream in an imaginary world at the former home of great writer Lu Xun, discover the secrets of tea therapy, and glide along the centuries-old canals on a Chinese gondola.

The Hadrian's Wall Country Partnership in Northeast England is good example of bringing branding, product development and visitor information under a common theme. The development of an 80 mile footpath, the Hadrian's Wall Country Bus service, interpretive programs and themed events, all based in and around this World Heritage site has helped to unite the region to deliver brand experiences that cross many districts and local government boundaries.

PLACEMAKING

It is easy for residents of any community to overlook the appearance of their streets, the absence of trees, the poor lighting, trash and bad signage that may have evolved over the years. Visitors, however, are much less forgiving. Where attention has been paid to the aesthetics of a place, including preserving or enhancing its natural qualities and environments, it gains the reputation as a "special place" or a "fun place to hangout," and this goes a long way toward supporting the brand.

The provision of attractive, vibrant, and safe locations provides a distinctive sense of place to complement the brand strengths and main attractors of the city.

Placemaking describes the practice of creating, administering and managing this public environment so that it provides attractive and rewarding experiences for residents and visitors. The provision of attractive, vibrant, and safe locations offers a distinctive sense of place to complement the brand strengths and main attractors of the city. Placemaking can involve parks, streetscapes, public art, wayfinding, landscaping and public amenities and is implemented through place management programs inspired by the brand. Even when they are not inspired by the brand it is vital that they be of the highest standard.

Hakon Iversen, Chairman at the Nordic Urban Design Association, is a strong advocate for the role of branding in urban design. "Place branding, integrated urban design, and placemaking are all about people, the content, and the stories a place needs to tell in order to attract others to it. It makes sense for us to draw inspiration from the authentic brand of a place when we are designing and enhancing its public spaces. As urban designers, this helps us understand and appreciate the qualities and heritage of place in the design process."

Placemaking can act as an important catalyst in attracting, holding and dispersing people throughout the city. It provides an ambiance, feel and appearance that marks the place as being special and different from other options. It creates the type of place where people want to simply "hangout" and spend time. A city's sense of place is strongly influenced by the focus and enthusiasm of city government. For some cities, a more holistic view is taken where urban design and architecture are integral to the brand identity. This has happened in Ogdensburg NY, Portland OR, Bilbao (Spain), Holon (Israel), and Belfast Downtown-Waterfront(Ireland).

On the Aegean Sea, Turkey's third largest city, Izmir has an ambitious goal of transforming many of its public spaces in order to rebuild Izmir's image and reinvent its identity. These major urban design and redevelopment projects are being conducted by the government and private sector with the objective of establishing Izmir as a world city.

Visitors to Anaheim CA can sense the Disney experience long before they arrive at the gates of the Disneyland theme park. The precinct that surrounds the theme park is fastidious about easy access, readily accessible free transportation, clear wayfinding and signage, and its strong sense of welcome. Bronze maps of the precinct have been inlaid into the sidewalk at intersections surrounding the park to assist pedestrians to easily find their way around.

Strict design codes for buildings, landscaping, and streetscapes are employed by Carmel CA, Cannon Beach OR, and Peggy's Cove, Nova Scotia (Canada) to ensure that they retain their distinctiveness and reputations as idyllic seaside communities.

Wayfinding

Signage and wayfinding systems serve vital roles. They not only inform, guide, and motivate visitors and residents, they also provide attractive and functional expressions of the brand. They help shape the identity of a place through their style, design, colors, lettering, content and placement. Effective wayfinding can contribute significantly toward the satisfaction of residents and visitors in urban locations. They can also play an important role in encouraging people to spend time and money in one place rather than another.

First coined in the 1960s, the word wayfinding has become an integral part of urban planning and placemaking. It is the art and science of moving people through an environment to a desired location using a number of visual cues including, but not limited to, directional signage, place identification, streetscaping, visual landmarks and many forms of environmental graphics. Figure 7 provides examples of some of these elements. Wayfinding design combines the disciplines of graphic design, architecture, storytelling, industrial design and landscape architecture. Simply put, it is the design and application of visual communications in the built world.

Todd Mayfield, principal of Axia Creative, captured the vital link between wayfinding and place branding in saying, "In addition

Images provided by Axia Creative (All rights reserved 2012) axiac.com

Figure 7: Wayfinding Elements

to helping visitors navigate through a place, wayfinding can help support a brand. Where advertising and marketing communications make a brand promise, wayfinding will help keep it by packaging an environment with brand-supportive graphics."

Retail and leisure environments thrive when visitors can easily find their way there. Districts and neighborhoods become popular destinations when a brand-supportive wayfinding system illuminates a clearly marked path for patrons. With the proper combination of planning, design and branding, a wayfinding system can be as beautiful as it is functional. It will enhance the character of an area by creating a memorable sense of place for visitors and the local community, thus presenting an attractive backdrop for the delivery of brand experiences.

The Brand Manual and Guidelines

Call it the brand manual, handbook, blueprint, toolkit, strategy or guidelines – it doesn't really matter. What does matter is that it provides the guidelines outlining how to accurately project the brand identity and how to deliver the city's distinctive and compelling experiences. Importantly, it's more than simply the usage and technical guidelines for the logo. It documents the rationale behind the brand, defines how the brand should be adopted and used, and how it should be managed and evaluated over time.

Many cities have online brand centers providing partners with ready access to the manual and updated information relating to their brand. I never cease to be amazed by the number of brand guidelines that do not provide any description of what the brand is, or the rationale behind it. They often only contain the specifications for how to use the visual design system. It is little wonder that so many of these efforts falter when there is no brand rationale, product development or clear path for partners and stakeholders to support the delivery of the brand promise.

Questions

- Do communications successfully answer the customer's perennial *What's in it for me?* question?
- Has the Destination Promise™ been correctly and creatively expressed?
- How well is the brand delivered at all critical touchpoints?
- Are the principles of integrated marketing being used?
- Are the streets and public spaces welcoming, attractive and present positive experiences?
- Is the city easy to navigate as a motorist and pedestrian?
- Are the brand strategy and guidelines readily available for partners?

CHAPTER THIRTEEN

Step Six: Adoption – How Do We Maximize the Support of Stakeholders?

Walt Disney said, "You can dream and create the most wonderful place in the world, but it takes passionate people to make the dream a reality." That may explain why Disney doesn't have staff, it has more than 100,000 cast members who create the Disney Magic. Walt recognized that if Frontierland, Main Street, and the Pirates of the Caribbean were going to delight millions of guests it would take dedicated, skilled, trained, and enthusiastic partners to create the "*Happiest Place on Earth.*"

While there are many tools in a brand manager's arsenal, as there are for Disney, it is people who are ultimately the most influential and credible communicators of brand experiences. Behind the scenes, it takes people to drive the strategies, decisions, designs, creativity, management, systems, and policies that influence communications and the customer experiences. They may be marketers, engineers, business and civic leaders, educators, and service professionals. In the case of a community it also takes political leaders, retailers, entrepreneurs, investors, and front line staff to develop a compelling and sustainable brand.

As the Disney experience shows, only people can fulfill a brand promise and be responsible for its ongoing vitality. They must be true to the Destination Promise™ and breathe life into the many touchpoints that add value and create those memorable and satisfying experiences for customers. According to Brian Hall, Chief Marketing Officer at the St. Louis Convention & Visitors Commission, "Enlisting the support of the entire community is key to fulfilling our brand promise as a cosmopolitan, world-class experience that is all within reach. To accomplish this, we offer training programs free-of-charge and have inspired thousands of St. Louisans on the value of tourism and what it means to be proud ambassadors of this community."

Buy-in Should Have Started Months Ago!

We know of countries, cities and regions that have launched a new brand with great fanfare, only to see it fall flat. Key stakeholders didn't support it because it was developed behind closed doors with little or no consultation with anyone outside of the DMO. Instead, they should have been working to avoid this situation by building understanding, buy-in and support from the start of the project.

This early buy-in will help to orchestrate a 'soft landing' for the brand and it will be well received, endorsed, and supported by key public, non-profit, and private sector organizations, stakeholders and trade partners.

Who Should Be Involved?

The successful implementation of the brand strategy will require actions by more than just the City Council or CVB. It requires the long-term advocacy, passion, and support of dozens, and maybe hundreds, of local individuals and organizations.

The most potent brand might call for changes in behavior and relationships for the lead organization, its Board, and partners.

Just as during the Middle Ages when the entire village contributed to building the city's cathedral, today it takes the whole village to build and sustain the city brand. It took generations of masons, laborers, glassmakers, and carpenters to build a cathedral over hundreds of years. When building a city brand, just about everyone has a role to play because they can strengthen or weaken it whenever they, or their work, comes in contact with the city's customers.[27]

Successful brand planning can be very much about change management and cities periodically falter because embracing these principles can prove difficult. The most potent brand might call for changes in behavior and relationships for the lead organization, its Board, and partners in order to build a compelling and sustainable brand from the inside out. It may require variations to structures, systems, recruitment, processes, attitudes, and "the way we do things around here."

There are possibly hundreds of prospective brand partners, stakeholders, and interested parties across the city. Ongoing education and information is essential to maintain their focus, both as a refresher and because there is frequent staff turnover in so many positions that affect the brand communications and delivery. For some, such as local government, DMO, Chamber of Commerce, and the tourism industry, the brand should be central to their mission. There are others such as media, developers, real estate agents, and service staff who project a positive, and sometimes inadvertently a negative or dated, image of the city who also need to understand the brand and your mission – and how it relates to them.

Some individuals such as politicians, sports stars, business leaders, and celebrities often find themselves in the role of city ambassador, whether they set out to be or not. Hotels, attractions, tour operators, and others are also actively trying to entice people to the city. And we can't forget about the universities and colleges, retailers, developers, and employers. Each of them may tell outsiders to visit, invest, relocate or study in the area – all with different messages and intent.

The Adoption Strategy

The number one objective at this point is to encourage understanding, adoption and correct use – one brand, many partners, one voice. The adoption strategy should outline the goals, techniques, and messages that will boost support and use of the brand by relevant stakeholders. It calls for you to identify and prioritize the individuals and organizations most important to the health of the brand and allow them to initiate the actions needed to support the brand. The leading adoption goals will encourage stakeholders to:

- Understand the brand benefits and rationale
- Know how it affects their role and everyday responsibilities of their organization
- Understand how they can support and use the brand
- Consider how they can make on-brand behavior easier
- Deliver outstanding experiences to support the brand

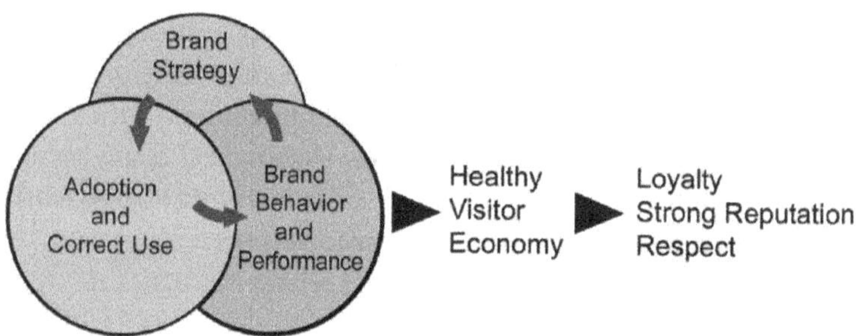

Figure 8: The Destination Brand Loyalty Process

Figure 8 demonstrates the benefits that come to a destination from broad stakeholder adoption and how on-brand behavior leads to loyalty, respect and a place with a strong reputation and healthy visitor economy – and ideally setting in place a virtuous upward spiral.

Wendy Hielsberg at the Oshkosh CVB says, "The local media played a huge role in encouraging the community to embrace our brand and generate support for the CVB. Whenever Oshkosh secures a new event or attendances increase, the media now recognizes our brand positioning as *Wisconsin's Event City* and its pivotal role in securing this business. This generates a great sense of community pride because the media is talking about the great role we are playing and this continues to stimulate buy-in. This probably wouldn't have happened had we not engaged senior executives in the media from the earliest days of the project."

In order to directly engage stakeholders and partners throughout the Rogue Valley (OR), Travel Medford conducted its launch event in the form of an innovative roadshow that lasted a full day and traveled forty miles to five locations in the region. Anne Jenkins from Travel Medford explains their rationale, "Our brand is based on *great performances daily* and we wanted to show that the brand belongs to everyone in the region. We conducted an outreach to actors, artisans, winemakers, and artists even in the small towns who will bring our brand to life. Conducting the launch this way has enabled us to accelerate the adoption and support of the brand and gained great kudos for us in going to them."

Ready to Launch!

The successful launch of the brand is essential to its long term viability. One of the keys to a successful rollout is to carefully plan the many actions needed to orchestrate an impactful launch. You may only get one chance to generate the enthusiasm, support and energy needed for acceptance. Consequently, the launch should not be approached in an ad hoc or casual manner, most importantly when there are tangible examples of the brand deployment in use.

It is particularly important that staff, partners and stakeholders understand the rationale behind the brand and the level of community consultation that has taken place.

There are no definitive rules for conducting public launch or announcement of a city brand strategy. Some prefer to keep everything under wraps until a wide range of marketing applications can be revealed at the same time with great fanfare, while others choose to have a "soft" launch by revealing the main elements of the brand with an explanation of how it was developed, and then release various elements over the following months. Whichever path you choose, you should have prototypes to demonstrate how various applications are likely to look. And of utmost importance is ensuring that the budget for the project is not misconstrued as having been spent for only a new tagline and logo. This fact is often misrepresented in media reports.

Be sure that staff, partners and stakeholders understand the rationale behind the brand, the level of community consultation that has taken place, and what it means to them and their job. Support for a place brand is always enhanced when constituents know that the process was inclusive and not created behind closed doors by "the usual suspects." Be sure to acknowledge the efforts of individuals who aided in the development phases and particularly give credit to those who made extraordinary contributions. No doubt your Brand Advisory Committee deserves special kudos.

After the completion of the Durham NC brand strategy, CVB executives conducted sixty face-to-face meetings with government, community, business, and education leaders across the community. This enabled the CVB to not only promote a clear understanding of the brand, but also stimulate wide community acceptance and its use by groups as diverse as Duke University, the Research Triangle Park, the Durham Bulls baseball team and neighborhood organizations.

John Cooper, President of Yakima Valley VCB in Washington advises, "Plan to carefully orchestrate the launch with a detailed plan that includes media and community relations, the event launch format, and stakeholder briefings. Give consideration to who should speak at the launch and who the best spokespersons are to publicly lend their support to the effort. We found it very valuable to meet with the editorial boards of newspapers and to treat all media equally in distributing information about the brand." Cooper adds, "No matter how much research, consultation and agreement there may have been, be prepared for the criticisms and possible misunderstandings. It pays to do your homework and prepare for the inevitable barbs with responses (which in some cases may be no response at all). Be sure that prime stakeholders are informed and are also ready to respond to possible criticisms with the suggested talking points. Encourage them to hold tight and ride out possible storms that some love to stir."

Bruce Dickson, a community consultation planner at Tourism Development Solutions, also advises, "Don't over-react to the vocal locals when you launch a new initiative. They may possess different names in different countries – naysayers, full-time cynics, or whiners, but their perpetually negative outlook and destructive power can derail projects. We all know who they are, a small handful who make it their mission to publicly campaign against and actively undermine new visions, new projects, and even change itself. To keep a project on track, the best response to their unyielding cynicism is to ignore them and wisely move on. Certainly weigh up their arguments but don't allow them to derail the project. Their predictable views should never be confused with the legitimate concerns of others. Those perspectives should always be considered."

Wendy Hielsberg at the Oshkosh CVB agrees with this sentiment saying, "The one aspect I was not prepared for after the brand launch was some of the negative comments. We were so focused on the launch and developing the brand applications. I had to learn not to take the few negative criticisms personally. Change like this is most often met with resistance. We continued to successfully implement the brand and shortly the negativity went away and was replaced with praise and support. Be sure to get the brand right, prepare for possible negative reactions – but be patient!"

In stark contrast to many places, the Canadian Tourism Commission launched its new brand in stages stretching over more than a year and a half. The Brand Canada team began by launching brand rationale, followed by the tagline (Canada. Keep

Exploring.) some six months later, and didn't reveal the logo and visual identity for almost another year. As a result, the brand was well understood and already widely adopted by the industry by the time the logo launched. By releasing elements of the brand in deliberate stages, the CTC forced people to listen and think, and not just react.

Residents and Leaders as Brand Ambassadors

The most important ambassadors for cities are its current and past residents. They have great credibility and a capacity to convey positive sentiments to audiences of importance to the city. Their passionate support for the city can be far more influential than paid advertising and marketing programs.

Brand ambassadors are people who are engaged to represent the place in a positive, influential and accurate manner. Some are appointed and some might be paid, but most are volunteers. In some cases, places have engaged well-known local personalities or famous people with ties to the city to endorse and represent it. Irrespective of the available budget, a well-managed ambassador program can positively influence external perceptions. For instance, with people everywhere suffering from information overload, a message has more credibility when it is delivered by a known source. Cities would be well advised to tap into professional networks of local organizations and residents to rally support for representing the place to outside audiences. This is supported by research conducted by New York-based Development Counsellors International. Their research revealed that "dialogue with industry peers" is the most important source of information that influences perceptions of a city's business climate among the business community.

At Sheffield, England's brand launch event, the city's leading firms were provided with an ambassador toolkit which encouraged them to sell Sheffield in a more synchronized way. This encouraged businesses, educational institutions and cultural organizations to work with the city's marketing and tourism groups to tell Sheffield's stories.

Louisville KY's brand strategy was founded on the premise of it being *Possibility City*. The strategy was designed to raise its profile nationally as a destination for visitors, talent and business, and to encourage champions within the community to step forward. In addition to a series of humorous television ads targeting locals, a 'Friends of Lou' website was created as a meeting place for people far and wide who love *Possibility City* and who want to share their pride in it. The budget has been cut as a result of the recession, but the 'Friends of Lou' site is still active and has attracted over 100,000 supporters who continue to be keen ambassadors for the city.

In support of its brand strategy, the Australian city of Wollongong also launched a campaign targeting residents and past students to encourage them to convey positive messages about the city. The name of the campaign, *We love the Gong* is a light-hearted play on the affectionate nickname of the city. The objective is to address and neutralize any negative perceptions of the city and encourage locals to share their love of the city and project it as an attractive place to visit, live and invest.

Brand Awareness Training

Some stakeholders and partners will require more in-depth brand education and training than others. Programs specifically related to communicating the brand, product development and delivering the brand should be custom-designed for executives and business leaders, sales and marketing, and front-line personnel. It is possible that programs may also be needed for government organizations and departments to assist in aligning the brand with placemaking, planning, policy making and services. In some cases, it's beneficial to engage a qualified outside vendor to develop the brand awareness training programs.

The St. Louis MO Convention & Visitors Commission designed the brand awareness program *St. Lou is… Me* for staff at all levels of local organizations. It was created to empower executives, sales and front liners to own their guests' experiences by becoming

St. Louis ambassadors. An in-house trainer was recruited from Ritz Carlton Hotels to create and conduct the two hour training program which includes the background and benefits of the brand, how to answer guest questions, address misperceptions about the city, and city trivia. Importantly, taxi drivers (an important touchpoint for every city) must do the training to gain their licenses.

The Flinders Ranges in South Australia developed several types of brand awareness training programs for tour operators, enabling them to better understand the Ediacaran fossil discovery, local flora and fauna, the geology and uniqueness of the region, and the importance of the brand strategy so that they can develop more innovative products and deliver high quality experiences. This was achieved through face-to-face and small group training, training materials, networking opportunities and familiarization visits to the area.

Questions

- Have you developed detailed plans for the launch?
- Who should be involved? What do they need to know? What do you want them to do?
- Have you considered the policies, regulations and roles that may need to be changed?
- Is it clear how partners can adopt and use the brand?

CHAPTER FOURTEEN

Step Seven: Action and Afterward – How Do We Keep the Brand Fresh?

Your job isn't over after the launch – in fact, it's just beginning! Place branding is long-term because it is an ongoing organizing and management tool that requires non-stop focus. You can't afford to get comfortable or complacent because it involves a constant battle to remain relevant and competitive. It doesn't take long for what may have been a thriving destination or city to lose favor or momentum and fall victim to trends that it did not pay attention to.

The sooner key stakeholders embrace the brand, the sooner the brand will thrive. It's long-term vitality depends on how the lead organization manages six issues. They are:

1. Brand Leadership
2. Brand Management
3. Brand Communications
4. Product Development and Experience Management
5. Placemaking
6. Monitoring and Evaluation

1. Brand Leadership

Successful brands are led from the top and owned at the grassroots by customers. This high level influence is termed brand leadership and provides the strategic focus and prioritization for long-term results, partnerships, and competitive advantage. Some of the brand leadership actions that should be considered are:

Brand Leadership Committee: A committee representing key partners should be maintained for at least the first few years after the brand is introduced. This group should raise community-wide awareness of brand related issues, build solutions where appropriate, and when necessary apply peer pressure for correct interpretation and support for the brand. It should also identify and address gaps in the delivery of the brand experiences. The committee should involve the Brand Manager and key staff, along with appropriate government and partner representatives.

The Brand Manager: This executive should be selected at the start of the process. It is his or her job to keep the brand on track and manage relationships. Brand management involves "inside out" actions focused on their organization and partners to influence how they think and act when projecting the brand. The brand manager must maintain a vigilant eye on all applications of the brand. While innovation and creativity are essential for a vibrant brand, there should be no tolerance for variations from the detailed guidelines in the brand manual. Just one small variation after another and suddenly you're way off strategy. Managing the brand involves much more than the technical oversight of logo and color usage. It calls for close attention to every critical communication and touchpoint with customers.

Strategic Planning: The brand should not be considered as simply an "add-on." It should be an integral element, as appropriate, in the strategies of all key organizations because they have an important role in its management and sustainability. This particularly applies to those in tourism where the brand should be central to everything they do.

Brand Champions: Great brands need people who will champion their cause. They are both internal and external catalysts for the vision, values, and brand development. The brand champions may be appointed ambassadors or spokespersons, or they may be individuals or organizations that advance the brand through their advocacy, funding and support. They could be in positions of authority or influence who command widespread respect and are prepared to passionately champion the brand at the highest levels.

Governance: One of the little recognized but most influential success factors in place branding is the quality and vitality of the Board of Directors of lead organizations, specifically DMOs. Many boards are unsure of their role and try to micromanage day to day activities, instead of being future-focused on long-term organization health, setting policies and opening doors for the organization at the highest levels. I recommend the excellent book, *Destination Leadership for Boards* by Bill Geist of Zeitgeist Consulting which provides practical solutions and insights into the special challenges confronting DMO and non-profit boards. [28]

2. Brand Management

Brand management is tactical and has a short-term focus, compared to the long-term focus of brand leadership. It should not happen by accident or through *ad hoc* efforts. It is about shaping and managing perceptions, satisfaction and opinions – and that's not easy! Periodically brand managers must re-energize partners, stakeholders, and even customers.

Brand management embraces more than the traditional marketing functions. It calls for every customer-facing aspect of the city to be aligned with the Destination Promise™. While the traditional view of branding may have been centered on advertising, public relations, sales and publications, today it extends to issues such as placemaking, wayfinding, infrastructure, visitor services, interpretation, partnerships, and experience development.

Brand Talent: Working under the direction of the brand manager should be a team of talented people, some of whom may be outside vendors and marketing specialists. These experts should be the best the organization can afford. Periodically, we see efforts to design a website, brochures and advertising by using a local graphic designer or staff member who doesn't have the necessary skills or experience. Just as you may go to the best medical specialist who may be out of town, you should also go to the best and most appropriate marketing vendors. If it means paying a bit more, the benefit to the community by way of extra economic activity will make it worthwhile.

3. Brand Communications

When the brand messages are consistently, correctly and creatively communicated to the right target audiences at the right time, they should trigger the desired emotions, appeal to customer logic, and enhance the brand image. Every person conveying brand messages must always ask the question, "Have I correctly and creatively reinforced the brand in this decision or activity?." This applies to every opportunity to reflect and reinforce the brand, whether selecting a photographic image, choosing the color of carpet for a trade show booth, or proofing copy for a publication or website.

While your city might have outstanding communications programs, the most unexpected events can cause a setback for your brand. Every day there are stories of disasters, corruption, epidemics and accidents that overturn the great work of communities. There is no escaping the fact that bad things do happen to good places. Every city needs a crisis communications plan to protect its brand equity and reputation. "This has never been more important," notes Peggy Bendel, President of Bendel Communications International and author of *It's a Crisis! Now What?* "Though you can't know when a crisis may strike, it's near-inevitable that you'll face one sooner or later. Plan ahead: even the smallest city can develop a basic crisis communications plan." [29]

4. Product Development and Experience Management

To remain relevant and in demand, product development, placemaking and experience management should receive the same level of focus as communications and sales. This requires city-wide collaboration involving ongoing evaluation, innovation and discussions with experience providers, prospective investors, partners and residents to canvas ideas and implement programs aligned with the brand. One of the best ways to tackle this is through the designation of a City Brand Experience Committee that includes key private, public and nonprofit members. Engagement in product development should not be an afterthought for the DMO, but should be integral to its mission, marketing, and links to economic development and investment.

5. Placemaking

The ways in which the city's visitors, residents and organizations interact with its public spaces, streetscapes and gateways is critical to the success of every place brand. The brand manager, along with the City Brand Experience Committee, should work closely with city officials to ensure that there is a synergistic relationship between the urban domain and the needs of the city's customers. The degree to which the public domain is inspired by the city's brand will depend upon the degree that city planners, architects, urban planners, landlords, developers, and elected leaders are engaged, understand the strategy, and adopt it. This calls for ongoing commitment and collaboration between these groups.

6. Monitoring and Evaluation

With the brand now launched, it's vital to closely monitor and manage its progress and make adjustments when necessary. This doesn't have to be an expensive or time-consuming exercise. While several performance measures such as visitor numbers, information requests received, lodging tax revenue, occupancy levels, visitor spending, and advertising responses may already be monitored, there are several other brand health metrics that should be appraised at least once a year.

Brad Dean of Myrtle Beach Area Chamber of Commerce gives valuable advice in saying, "We have seen considerable success in defining our brand as how our consumers desire it, placing great emphasis on affordability and value, and marrying that brand to a results-oriented, strategic marketing plan. We determine not one singular way but instead agree on several ways to measure our success, including measuring visits to our website or national media coverage garnered and many, many others. By taking such an integrated and detailed approach, we can manage the branding process more carefully, stay hands-on, and keep our key stakeholders on board and tuned in to the progress we're making in reaching desired outcomes."

On-going research is also a high priority for the brand management of Durham CVB. Shelly Green, CEO explains, "We conduct a variety of public opinion and satisfaction surveys to monitor the brand and ensure that it continues to be relevant and respected by both internal and external audiences. This helps us keep the customer and the performance of our visitor experiences front and center in our decision-making."

Monitor the following six indicators to ensure that your brand remains relevant and meaningful over time.

1. Stay focused on the demographics, behavior and satisfaction of target audiences.
2. Ensure that your positioning and Destination Promise™ remain meaningful.
3. Ensure that core experiences are relevant and high quality.
4. Monitor touchpoints to ensure that they are aligned with customer needs and reflect the brand.
5. Keep the visual identity elements and communications fresh and creative.
6. Watch trends that influence demand and behavior.

Some of the criteria and methods for use when evaluating the brand, beyond the normal visitor performance measures include:

Performance Indicator	Method
Brand adoption by stakeholders	Review commercial, government, cultural and community organizations to gauge the extent of their adoption of the brand – beyond the logo and tagline use. Consider the content and accuracy of brand elements in publications, websites and other communications
Community pride and brand support	Conduct a survey of residents, businesses, tourism, and government organizations. Repeat every two years.
Co-operative support	Track the level of participation in the city's co-operative marketing.
Customer profiles	Assess shifts in customer profiles and source markets.
Customer satisfaction	Conduct ongoing customer surveys to monitor satisfaction with your experience delivery.
Brand consistency	Review the appearance and content of all marketing materials that project the city including those produced outside of the area, e.g. tour operators, websites.
Media coverage	Monitor the media for use of desired brand messages.
Stakeholder feedback	Survey key stakeholders, partners, and city messengers to review and monitor brand development issues.
Attitudes toward the city	Monitor shifts in customer attitudes, perceptions, and image of the city.

Questions

- Is the brand completely integrated into key city organizations?
- Are structure, process, and recruitment policies tied to the brand?
- Is an annual brand audit conducted?

APPENDIX

Place Branding Glossary

The following terms and definitions may assist with understanding the concepts of place branding.

Brand: A brand is the source of a distinctive promise for customers from a product, service or place. Everything the lead organization does in collaboration with its partners and community should be oriented around delivering and constantly enhancing this promise.

Brand Architecture: This defines the relationships, structure and links between a city brand's internal and external locations and partners.

Brand Associations: These associations (positive and negative) are what customers think of when they hear or see the city's name, tagline, or symbols. In the case of Las Vegas, these may include desert, hot, The Strip, neon signs, gambling, etc.

Brand Awareness: The degree to which the city's name is present in the minds of prospective customers. When exposed to the name, people should immediately recognize it and form positive associations.

Brand Culture: Brand culture brings the brand to life by aligning with the brand and getting all stakeholders "on the same page." It enables the place to deliver its Destination Promise™.

Brand Equity: The accumulated loyalty, awareness, and financial value of the brand that is accrued over time.

Brand Essence: The "heart and soul" or DNA of the brand. It should be a short phrase that is concise and rich in meaning, e.g. Las Vegas could be "adult freedom."

Brand Identity: The brand identity comprises the unique set of visual, auditory, and other stimuli that project the brand through its many applications in order to shape market perceptions. These include the attributes, benefits, logo, fonts, tagline, and colors.

Brand Image: How the brand is perceived from the customer's point of view.

Brand Loyalty: This is often considered the single most important outcome of a branding strategy. It may be best measured through repeat transactions, referrals, and spending patterns.

Brand Management: These actions ensure that the brand's value and promises are maintained and consistently delivered.

Brand Partners: These individuals and organizations are responsible for funding, communicating and delivery of the city's brand.

Brand Personality: This describes the place using human personality traits. Las Vegas traits may be fun loving, gregarious, flamboyant and indulgent. They are the character of the place.

Brand Platform: The brand platform is the foundation on which the Destination Promise™ and all future brand experiences will be based. It includes the brand vision, values, benefits and personality.

Brand Portfolio: For a place, the portfolio may refer to tourism, economic development, education, investment, and relocation activities that benefit from the city's reputation and identity.

Brand Positioning: Brand positioning establishes what we want customers to think and feel about the place. It relates to the position in consumer's minds (and hearts) that we want to occupy.

Brand Values: These are the principles that the city and its constituents believe in and live by. They are the guiding principles by which residents want their community to develop.

Brand Vision: It clarifies the high-level role that the brand will play in assisting the city achieve its long-term vision and goals.

Community Brand: Created to resonate with local residents and is usually designed to boost local pride, provide a sense of identity for the place or increase resident patronage for local residential, retail, entertainment, leisure and sporting activities.

Destination Brand: Also referred to as a "tourism brand," it is a brand founded on the location being an attractive place to visit.

Destination Promise™: This encapsulates the positioning, benefits and values that distinguishes the place from competitors. It acts as a vision and roadmap to deliver superior value to customers.

DMO: A destination marketing organization may also be referred to as a destination management organization. In the context of this book it is used as shorthand for Convention & Visitors Bureaus, Chambers of Commerce, local government entities, downtown associations, economic development authorities and other similar organizations responsible for the marketing of a city or destination.

Economic Development Brand: Sometimes referred to as an "investment brand" it is directed toward business relocation, expansion and investment, and may not always include tourism.

Key Experiences: These are the encounters that underpin your positioning and Destination Promise™.

Overarching Place Brand: This is a holistic brand encompassing all aspects of the city's marketing portfolio. It may also be called a domain, all of place, or umbrella brand.

Placemaking: This is the act of creating and managing the public environment so that it provides attractive and rewarding experiences for residents and visitors.

Sense of Place: Those elements that create a feeling that a location is a special place, distinct from anywhere else.

Touchpoints: These are the most critical and manageable moments or points where the customer comes in contact with the place and where its reputation can be enhanced or devalued.

Wayfinding: The systems of signs, markers, information and interpretation that enable people to understand and navigate places.

End Notes

1 European City Mayors: City Brands August 28, 2008

2 US Census Bureau, "Statistical Abstract of the United States," December 15, 2006,

3 BBC, "Should We Rebrand Britain?" (May 8, 2001)

4 American Marketing Association http://www.marketingpower.com/AboutAMA

5 Simon Anholt, *Competitive Identity* (Palgrave Macmillan; 1st edition, 2007)

6 Richard Florida *Who's your city?* (Basic Books, 2008)

7 Nigel Morgan et al. *Destination Branding* (Oxford: Butterworth Heinemann, 2002).

8 Antoinette Martin, "Selling Cities Despite Bad Images" (New York Times, August 22, 2008)

9 Maureen Littlejohn. "The Rebranding of CVB's and Leading the Change" (Convene, May 2005)

10 Amie Keeley, "Essex: County bids to rebrand its coastline" (EDAT Suffolk Magazine, June 14, 2011)

11 Rebecca Gardyn. "Packaging Cities," American Demographics Magazine, (January 2002)

12 Duane Knapp and Gary Sherwin, *Destination BrandScience* (DMAI, 2005)

13 National Trust for Historic Preservation, www.preservationnation.org

14 Neil Lee, "Ideopolis: Knowledge City-Regions Distinctiveness and Cities" (The Work Foundation 2008)

15 Sonia Krisnan. "In growing areas, a tale of too-similar cities" (The Seattle Times, September 19, 2006)

16 Whisper Brand Strategy Consultants, "Theory of Adulation," (January 14, 2006)

17 Civic Strategies Inc. "What Comes After Incorporation?" (September 23, 2006)

18 Development Counsellors International www.aboutdci.com

19 Geoff Ayling, *Rapid Response Advertising* (Business & Professional Publishing 1998.

20 Fort Worth Star Telegram November 8, 2005

21 DMAI, *The Future of Destination Marketing* (DMAI 2007)

22 Richard Florida, "America's Most Ridiculous City Slogans" (The Atlantic, May 23 2011)

23 KXAN News, "Austin Celebrates 20 Years of Live Music" (Aug 25, 2011)

24 BeatleNews.com Jan 17, 2012

25 Amadeus, *The Always-Connected Traveler* 2011

26 National Trust for Historic Preservation, "2010 Great American Main Street Awards"

27 Adapted from Marty Neumeier, *The Brand Gap*, (New Riders Publishing, 2003)

28 Bill Geist, Zeitgeist Consulting, *Destination Leadership for Boards*, (Neverland Publishing, November 2007)

29 Peggy Bendel, *It's A Crisis. Now What?*, (Sutherland House Publishing, April 2012)

With Thanks

I would like to thank the following friends and colleagues for their quotes, comments and advice that has assisted enormously in the research and writing of this book.

USA

Todd Mayfield	Axia Creative, formerly Mayfield Creative
Peggy Bendel	Bendel Communications International *Author: It's a crisis! Now what?*
Roger Brooks	Destination Development International
Andy Levine	Development Counsellors International
Shelly Green	Durham Convention & Visitors Bureau, North Carolina
Eric Aebi	Ethos Hospitality
Kerrie Walters	Grants Pass Visitors & Convention Bureau, Oregon
John Kelsh	Great Destination Strategies
Mary Klugherz	Great Destination Strategies
John Hope-Johnstone	HPR Internet & Social Media Marketing
Maura Gast	Irving Convention & Visitors Bureau, Texas
Brad Dean	Myrtle Beach Area Chamber of Commerce, South Carolina
Wendy Hielsberg	Oshkosh Convention & Visitors Bureau, Wisconsin
Misti Kerns	Santa Monica Convention & Visitors Bureau, California
Brian Hall	St. Louis Convention & Visitors Commission, Missouri
Ed Burghard	Strengthening Brand America

Derrick Daye	The Blake Project
Bruce Dickson	Tourism Development Solutions
Kari Westlund	Travel Lane County, Oregon
Anne Jenkins	Travel Medford, Oregon
Phil Bruno	Treat 'Em Right!
John Cooper	Yakima Valley Visitors & Convention Bureau, Washington
Bill Geist	Zeitgeist Consulting *Author: Destination Leadership for Boards*

International

Alastair Morrison, Ph.D.	Belle Tourism International Consulting, China
Joao Freire	Brandia, Portugal
Keith Dinnie, Ph.D.	Breda University of Applied Sciences, The Netherlands *Author: Nation Branding and City Branding*
Nigel Morgan	Cardiff Metropolitan University – Wales *Author: Destination Branding and Destination Brands*
John King	Global Travel & Tourism, Australia
Malcolm Allan	Colliers International, England
Marcus Osborne	FusionBrand, Malaysia
Robert Govers	Leuven University – Belgium *Author: Place Branding* and the *International Place Branding Yearbook*
Hakon Iversen	Nordic Urban Design Association, Norway
Mahesh Enjeti	SAI Marketing Counsel, Australia
Rodney Harrex	Tourism Australia, U.K.
Peter Valerio	Tourism Strategy Development Services, Australia
Tom Buncle	Yellow Railroad, Scotland, *Author: Handbook on Tourism Destination Branding*

About the Author

Bill Baker is President of Total Destination Marketing, and is recognized internationally as a thought-leader, author, speaker and for his pioneer work in branding places of all sizes, from nations to small cities. He has more than 30 years place branding and marketing experience in 25 countries.

Bill has created marketing and branding strategies that have involved hundreds of cities and regions. He has been directly involved in some of the most respected and successful destination branding campaigns in the USA, including Australia's highly acclaimed *Shrimp on the Barbie*, which he directed for seven years. He also produced tourism strategies for the Sydney 2000 Olympic Games and has assisted places throughout the USA, Australia, Europe and Canada. Bill has provided strategic counsel to several countries including Australia, Hong Kong, India, Macau, and Saudi Arabia.

He has been interviewed by CNN, The Travel Channel, New York Times, Los Angeles Times, Wall Street Journal, and many other media outlets worldwide. He is always in demand as a speaker on place branding where he energizes seminars and educational forums in the USA and abroad.

After having lived on three continents, Bill now resides in Portland, Oregon with his wife Joan and daughters, Renee and Kate.

If you would like information on Bill's availability to speak at your conference or seminar, visit: www.DestinationBranding.com/speaking.

To contact Bill email BillB@DestinationBranding.com.

Place Branding Education and Coaching Programs

Is it time to accelerate your brand planning or implementation efforts? We provide a variety of "how-to" programs specifically designed to meet the needs of small cities and regions. Many of the programs are based on the principles presented in this book.

Our *Place Brand Coaching Workshop* for your Board, marketing committee or city leaders is designed to fast track improvements to your city's competitiveness and branding efforts. Led by TDM President, Bill Baker a *Place Brand Coaching Workshop* lays the groundwork for the brand planning process. Whether you intend to conduct the planning yourself or engage a specialist firm, this energizing and insightful workshop is a wise investment. It will ensure that your leaders understand the concepts and pitfalls involved and are able to make well-informed decisions at critical milestones. Importantly, it encourages common understanding of place branding – what it is, how it works, and its benefits for your community and partners.

A *Place Brand Coaching Workshop* can be customized for sessions ranging from two to eight hours. In addition to demystifying place branding, Bill will lead discussions specific to your city during the second part of the Workshop.

Bill also conducts customized intensive two day *Place Branding Master Class seminars* for cities and regions worldwide. This intensive how-to seminar follows the 7A Destination Branding Process and provides attendees with an understanding of the tools and techniques to use in their brand planning. It includes an examination of the actions taken by successful place brands around the world, how to define a brand platform, how to unify stakeholders and how to deliver outstanding brand experiences. The overall focus of the Master Class is to address the issues that are critical for you to build a successful brand that will provide a sustainable competitive edge.

Bill is also available as a key note speaker for conferences and seminars on a wide range of topics relating to successful place branding and competitiveness.

For more information visit
www.DestinationBranding.com